TRUTH UNCHANGED, UNCHANGING

TRUTH UNCHANGED, UNCHANGING

D. MARTYN LLOYD-JONES

EVANGELICAL PRESS OF WALES

© D.M. Lloyd-Jones, 1950
First published (by Fleming H. Revell Co., USA), 1950
First British edition (by James Clarke & Co., Ltd), 1951
Reprinted 1956
Second (paperback) edition (by Evangelical Press), 1969
Reprinted 1973
Third edition (by the Evangelical Press of Wales), 1990
ISBN 1 85049 053 8

Cover photograph: Cwmtudu, near New Quay, Dyfed
(Ron & Phil Davies, Aberaeron)

Published by the Evangelical Press of Wales
Bryntirion, Bridgend, Mid Glamorgan CF31 4DX
Printed by Billing & Sons Ltd., Worcester

CONTENTS

To my
MOTHER
and the
memory of my
FATHER

PREFACE

THE PROBLEM OF THE PLACE AND VALUE OF APOLOGETICS in the presentation of the Christian faith at the present time is, clearly, one which cannot be discussed in a brief preface like this. None, however, can well deny that there is real and positive value in exposing the hollowness of mere clichés, and in demonstrating that what often passes as the hall-mark of learning is nothing but sheer prejudice.

I have tried in these lectures to make such exposé and demonstration by analysing some of the commoner assumptions on which so many to-day base their rejection of the Christian faith.

I trust that my comments will be of value not only to those who hitherto have been blinded by such assumptions, but also to many Christians who often seem to be needlessly brow-beaten by those who hurl at them the popular slogans of the hour. That my lines encourage and strengthen the latter, and provide them with ammunition in the fray, is my confident hope.

The five chapters of this book constitute the first series of the Jonathan Blanchard Lectures founded and instituted by the Alumni Association of Wheaton

College, Wheaton, Illinois. With a few minor changes, they were delivered there in the Orlinda Childs Pierce Chapel, August 11-15, inclusive, 1947.

Dr. Carl F. H. Henry, the President of the Association, when he did me the great honour of inviting me to be the first lecturer under this new foundation, indicated that he and his colleagues desired that these lectures should be of a general apologetic character.

I think it will be agreed that, whatever the deficiencies of the lectures, they certainly conform to that general desideratum.

I shall never forget the happy days spent at Wheaton, and all the kindness and hospitality shown to me and my family. My gratitude to my friend, Ted M. Benson, the genial and stimulating Secretary of the Alumni Association, is beyond words.

May Wheaton continue to produce alumni whose one ambition will be to "earnestly contend for the faith"!

D. M. L.-J.

Westminster Chapel,
London.

PREFACE TO THE THIRD EDITION

DR. LLOYD-JONES NEVER SAW HIMSELF AS AN apologist, but this little volume demonstrates his ability to present an apologetic for the gospel whenever he regarded this approach as appropriate.

The Apostle Peter exhorted us to "give a reason for the hope that is in you": these lectures should enable every Christian to do just that. Not even the greatest non-Christian intellect can be reasoned into the kingdom of heaven, but, inevitably, the gospel of the glorious God, who is the source of reason, must be rational. Thomas Aquinas saw this very clearly: when reason reaches its limit, there must be faith—his now famous "leap into the dark"—but once the leap is made, the faith can be seen to be reasonable.

The ancient Greek intellectuals had deified reason by calling it the Logos. The New Testament has revealed to all men that the Logos was made flesh— Jesus of Nazareth, the Son of God.

This book, like all the others by the same author, is about Him.

ANN DESMOND
(née Lloyd-Jones)

CHAPTER ONE

WHAT IS MAN?

WHAT IS MAN? ANY TRUE CONSIDERATION OF MAN and his problems in the modern world must answer that question. If the basic idea of what man is is a mistaken one, so of necessity will be the view of his troubles and what can be done for him. Now, here at the very commencement, we find that the modern popular view of man and his nature departs radically from the Biblical and Christian view, which up to approximately the last hundred years was almost universally believed and accepted. This modern view can be best described, perhaps, as the cult of self-expression, a view which has pervaded and influenced almost every department of life. It accounts for the most essential and characteristic aspects of modern behaviour. It is, for example, the true explanation of the last world war. This cult of self-expression, manifesting itself as the Nazi philosophy, was a large factor in leading Germany to plunge the world into that horror. It is a view based upon the claim that one has a right to express oneself even at the expense of others, and that what one likes is therefore of necessity legitimate. This same idea manifests itself in the realm of business, where the idea of salesmanship is largely based upon this philosophy of self-expression. It is to be seen likewise in the realm of education, where the old programme of teaching children the three Rs and the idea of discipline are no longer popular. The results of the present popular notion that the business of education is rather to train the child to express himself are to be seen on all hands both in the breakdown of parental control and in the increase of juvenile delinquency.

However, we shall be concerned, for our purposes, with this modern philosophy as it expresses itself particularly in the realm of religion and the world of the soul. Under the influence of this popular conception there has been during this present century a great and a radical change in the attitude of the average man and woman to the whole question of religion. Until the advent of this cult men were content to remain in a more or less negative position with respect to wrongdoing. Some freely admitted that they sinned and that there was no defence. Others tried to defend themselves by saying that the standards of religion were too high, the rules too stringent. Others, as a cloak for their sin, made great play with the love of God and His readiness to forgive. Still others talked about sin in terms of manliness, and posed as men who had broken through certain shackles and restraints. But, notwithstanding the manifold variations, the one central position common to them all was the admission of sin. They were all, in some way or another, defending themselves against their own consciences, and against the opinion of the Church and the Bible. The sum of their desire was to be left unattacked and uncondemned. Though that wish expressed itself sometimes, as we have seen, as an attack upon us on the grounds of a lack of manliness on our part, or of our being strait-laced, these malcontents did not say, and were not anxious to say, that we were wrong, though they longed that eventually we might be proved so. Their dearest desire was to protect themselves in some way or another against the charge of having gone astray. Sin, in general, was ashamed of itself. Though at times it tried in an aggressive manner to defend itself, the attitude was entirely negative.

The view of religion which is based upon this cult of self-expression is, on the other hand, thoroughly positive. Rather than defensive, its methods are offensive in character. Instead of resisting the attack of religion, it assails religion and all its adherents. Not content with trying to justify its ways, it commends itself as the only worthy way of life. It declares that the view of sin taught by the Church on the basis of the Bible, which has so long controlled the thought of the world, is not only inaccurate but actually perverted, and that when the Bible pleads with man to refrain from certain acts for his soul's sake, this book is indeed being his greatest enemy. All this old talk about sin, say the self-expressionists, is utterly foolish, leading to self-repression, which is, they aver, the only sin. What used to be called sin is just expression of self, the greatest and most vital possession that man has. Not to sin, according to the old meaning of the term, is to do violence to the greatest gift he possesses. They plead, therefore, for the abolition of the word "sin" in its earlier associations. Man, they say, is a creature possessing various powers, faculties, and instincts, and his highest good is to be found in the exercise of those powers. They point out as unhealthy perversion on the part of Christians the charge of iniquity and disgrace to society which formerly accompanied exhibitions of self-expression. They insist on the rightness of the natural and instinctive. They deplore what they term the tragic spectacle of mankind shackled against its highest good by adherence to the warnings of the Bible, the Church, and the saints. The advocates of this doctrine do not hesitate to follow this logic right to the end and to assert that the man who still believes in sin in the old way, and who therefore tries to discipline and to control his life, is a pervert, a psychopath who is not only sinning against himself and his own true destiny, but also against humanity at large. Thus it comes to pass, according to this view, that the greatest sinners in life have been those whom the various Churches have canonized as their greatest saints.

Such is the view of life espoused by countless thousands to-day in all countries. It is the view also that appeals to thousands more who are held back from fully accepting and yielding themselves to it, not because they see clearly that it is erroneous, but rather because they are restrained by a general spirit of fear, and by tradition. We can best consider this human view of life, and show its complete fallacy, by contrasting it with God's view as stated in the Bible. The teachings of our Lord and Saviour, Jesus Christ, are outspoken against sin. He said, "Wherefore if thy hand or thy foot offend thee, cut them off, and cast them from thee: it is better for thee to enter into life halt or maimed, rather than having two hands or two feet to be cast into everlasting fire. And if thine eye offend thee, pluck it out, and cast it from thee: it is better for thee to enter into life with one eye, rather than having two eyes to be cast into hell fire."[1] Now,

[1] Matt. xviii. 8, 9.

there we are reminded once more of the way in which every conceivable view of life and of men is invariably dealt with somewhere or another in the Scriptures. Modern man is constantly flattering himself and suggesting to himself that certain of his ideas are quite new. But here again we find an illustration of a view which prides itself on its modernity dealt with completely and exhaustively in the Bible.

The first criticism which we make of this modern cult of self-expression is that it fails to realize the true nature of self. It talks much about giving expression to self, and yet we can show very easily that its very ideas concerning that self are false, and do violence to man's true nature. Obviously, before expression must come definition; and, as we hope to show, our objection is not so much to the idea of self-expression *per se* as to the utterly false view of that self which is taken by so many to-day. The gospel answer to this modern cult is not a doctrine of repression, but rather a call to the realization of the true nature of the self. Now, the clash between the Biblical view and that of the moderns comes out very clearly in the quoted lines above, especially in the emphasis which Christ places on the word "thee." "If thine eye offend *thee* . . . cast it from *thee* . . . it is better for *thee* . . ." Let me put it to you in the form of two positive statements.

The modern view does not differentiate between the self and the various factors that tend to influence the self, the various factors which the self uses in order to express itself. Our Lord, on the other hand, draws that distinction very clearly and definitely in His emphasis on the word "thee." That He does so is perhaps the real cause of all the modern confusion. The view that is so popular to-day tends to regard man as a mere aggregate of various powers and forces which in their interaction produce a certain end result. Man in himself is but the resultant of these and their effects. What are these forces? Well, there is the very physical structure of the human body, and especially the various glands, notably the thyroid, pituitary, and suprarenal ductless glands, which tend to control some of the most vital functions. Normally, these glands are more or less perfectly balanced, but there are innumerable possible variations, and as one or the other tends to predominate, so the self, we are told, and the personality tend to vary. Probably we have all read statements which claim that all the great figures in history can be interpreted in terms of these slight variations in the relative proportions of the various glands which are to be found in their physical bodies. It is claimed that Shakespeare and Beethoven can thus quite easily be explained. According to this view, man is nothing but a biological mechanism, and his self, his personality, is purely the resultant of the interplay of biological forces. Closely allied with that theory is another, which tends to think of man rather in terms of what are called the instincts. Man, or the self, according to this view, is determined by the inter- action of the various instincts, or by the predominance of any one of a number of instincts, such as the herd instinct, the protective instinct, the fear instinct, the sex instinct, the hunger instinct. Man's essential per- sonality, his real self, is considered to be only the product of these forces. Another theory would lay great emphasis, in the analysis of the self, upon tradi- tion, surroundings, and upbringing. Here, the whole element of race, blood, and nationality comes in, and all the factors that can be traced to the social environ- ment and surroundings. There are still others, one of which tends to explain the self in more or less purely geographical or climatic terms. In this view the theology of a man like John Calvin is to be explained soley in terms of the fact that he lived in Switzerland. Northern races are said to be generally sterner and more inclined toward Calvinism in their doctrine, whereas one finds invariably that as one approaches the Equator, the doctrine tends to become increasingly Catholic in type.

We need not consider longer, however, the details of the various expressions of this modern man-made view. The important point to observe is that the self, as such, has become lost. It is no longer a distinct entity, but is regarded merely as the result produced by the interaction of various forces and factors. According to this theory, man is what he is entirely as the result of his glands, his instincts, his heredity, the particular climate in which he has been brought up; and his self-expression means allowing these factors to have free play and exercise in his conduct. Indeed, as he is just something composed of these factors, to restrain them means to do violence to him. By this logic it is fallacious to talk about the hand or the foot "offending," because the hand, the foot, and the eye constitute the real self. Here we come to the vital distinction. Though our Lord did not talk in terms of glands and instincts, did He not represent precisely the same thing in talking about the hands, the feet, and the eyes, which are but the external agencies of those other powers? But notice how He put the matter. He did not identify the self with these powers and instruments. It is distinct from them, greater than they, infinitely more important than they. They do not constitute self. They are simply the instruments and the servants which self is to control and to use according to its will. According to Christ, man is not a mere collection of biological forces. He is something infinitely greater. He is not a machine, nor is he an animal led and governed by whim. He is bigger than the body, bigger than tradition, history, and all else. For there is within man another element which transcends all these. This element is called the soul.

But we cannot leave our criticism of this false view of the self at this point; to do so would be to grant far too much to this modern idea. We can convict it not only of identifying the self with the various factors that tend to influence the self, but, further, of identifying it with only certain of those factors. Now, it is here we see what we must describe as the thorough dishonesty of this view, and what entitles us to say that it is nothing but an attempt to justify and to rationalize sin. Were it logical and thoroughgoing in the application of its own idea, we should at any rate respect it intellectually. But it is not, for it deliberately ignores that which does not suit its scheme and fit into its theory. For instance, it does not hesitate to brush aside what is called conscience, the sense of right and wrong which is within man, and for which man is no more responsible than he is for the other factors that these theorists emphasize. Conscience they try to dismiss as something false and extraneous which has been foisted and grafted upon man. Yet we all know that there is nothing more essentially and vitally a part of man than this very faculty. In the same way also there is the reasoning power, the power which above all others differentiates us from the animal. The animal is but a collection of the various powers and forces. He does not reason about them. He cannot think about them and consider what to do with them. The power to reason and to regard things objectively is peculiar to man. This intellectual power constantly urges him to pause and to consider, to deal with these other powers, controlling and harnessing them. But according to this modern cult the intellectual faculty is to be brushed aside and men are to behave and to live exactly as animals. The more they return to the animal level, the more truly are they expressing themselves. This was the view, for instance, of the late D. H. Lawrence, who taught that one of the greatest calamities that have ever afflicted the human race is the use of the mind and of reason. There are some instances, in fact, in which this exclusion of things which are inconvenient to the theory has been carried so far as to lead almost to the conclusion that the self is to be identified with nothing but the expression of the sex instinct and the gratification of the hunger instinct.

Thus we see that the whole modern view of self and of its real nature is sadly at fault. This view identifies the self with certain elemental forces in its make-up only, and therefore robs man of his greatest glory, his soul and his spirit, the sense in which he is independent of his body and all his powers, and greater than they. It is, therefore, an insult to him, something which would reduce him to the level of the beast, and ignore everything that is noblest and best and highest in human nature. Self-expression! Certainly! But what is man? A mere collection of impulses and instincts? No! Something infinitely more, something immeasurably bigger. An immortal soul with power to order and control those impulses and instincts, and to turn them to his use and service instead of being their slave. Not just hands, feet and eyes, but "thou," the self, a full personality. Have we realized this freedom in regard to ourselves?

We must consider as well how this cult of self-expression is inimical to the true and highest interests of the self. In a sense we have been dealing with that problem already, for, clearly, a view of the self which is hopelessly incomplete and inadequate, and which rules out everything which is best and most uplifting in man, must of necessity militate against the highest interests of our nature. But the word "offend" which was used by our Lord demands a further and a deeper consideration. The "thee," the self, is not only separate and distinct from hands, feet, and eyes, but may actually be "offended" by them. The various impulses and instincts that are within not only fail to constitute the true and only real self, but may actually be the greatest enemies of that self, sources of offence to it, causes of its damnation. Indeed, in order to safeguard that self, man is told that he may have to cut off a hand or pluck out an eye, and cast it from him. Here is something which the modern view entirely ignores; and it does so because its view of sin is false, failing to realize the danger that threatens self from within. The recognition of sin is really the crux of the whole matter. Were it not for sin, the teaching of self-expression would be adequate. Were man perfect as God made him, all the impulses and instincts would be working in the right direction and serving the highest interests of man. There would then be no problem; a man's life would be more or less automatic. It is sin and sins that have introduced a complexity into the life of man. The Bible mentions concupiscence, for instance, as a trait which dominates us all by nature, twisting and perverting acts which in and of themselves are quite right and pure. The very faculties and powers which were designed to be the servants of man have become his masters. But for sin, it would be legitimate for him to allow his impulses to guide him. Because of sin there is nothing so dangerous as to allow them to do so. Take once more the illustrations which our Lord gave in His statement. Think of the hand and the foot. What a useful instrument is the human foot! How obviously designed to benefit man! It is by walking that man goes about doing good; and yet it is with the same feet that he walks into places of vice and of evil repute and does harm to himself and others. Likewise the human hand. Think of all the good that is done with the hand. Think of a handshake, a pat on the back, a cup of cold water extended. Yet that self-same hand is quickly turned into a fist. Think of its striking another. Look at it and think of it as it fires a gun and commits murder. The hand as hand is perfect. But because of the effect of sin upon man it may become the instrument of his destruction. Likewise the human eye. What a wonderful instrument it is! It is incomparably greater in matters of delicacy and subtlety, of balance and refinement than any instrument ever invented by man. It is the organ with which the beauty of nature is appreciated, the smile on the face of a little child observed, the eyes of a loved one met. And yet it is this self-same organ which leads to lust, which is often the cause of grievous sin which frequently leads man to destruction. There is nothing iniquitous in the eye as such, but because of the effect of sin and its perverting influence, the eye, which is the most perfect instrument of all, may become the very cause of his damnation. Likewise, all the other forces, instincts, and powers that are within man, in and of themselves are harmless, but as the result of sin become a source of danger. How tragic it is therefore, and how foolish, to ignore sin! What an utterly false psychology! And yet that very principle is being advocated to-day. The whole fact of sin is being ignored; and the advice to give expression to self, therefore, is fraught with the most dangerous consequences conceivable.

Another way in which we can illustrate our contention that this view advocating subservience to impulses is inimical to the best interests of self, is by showing that it deliberately sets up but one standard of judgment. It has but one test of whether or not an act is right, the test of pleasure and enjoyment. Now, it is no part of the business of the gospel to denounce pleasure and enjoyment; in fact, the gospel offers a joy greater than anything else can ever give. But it is not content with testing by this one standard only. It desires to know the nature of the joys or the pleasures, whether it is good, whether it is true, and whether it is beautiful. Being really concerned about the highest interests of our nature, it naturally desires to avoid all risks, and realizes that we can never be too careful or too scrupulous in our examination. It knows that the child has but one test always, the test of pleasure and that alone. But it also knows what every father and mother knows, that what the child enjoys is often most harmful to it and may be thoroughly false and ugly. Men and women to-day do not like thought processes and discrimination. Like children, they desire to do what they like, and justify their actions on the grounds that they desire to do them and enjoy doing them. They therefore hate discipline and the facing of difficulty. They object to the inconvenience of having to face the questions of truth, goodness, evil, and beauty. They do what they want to do, pleading the rightness of self-expression. They have but one standard of value, that of pleasure. They do not ask whether their procedure is right, safe, or likely to administer to the development of their whole being, especially that which is highest and best in them. They are content with the one test only—is it enjoyable? How evident that this method is to revert to a state of childhood, or even to the condition of the jungle! Is not this utterly suicidal, judged by the true standard of human nature? If you desire to stifle your conscience, to murder your reason, and to quench every desire after higher and nobler things which arises in you, if you desire merely to satisfy the lust and the craving for pleasure, then go in for the modern cult. But if you desire the whole of yourself to be developed and expressed, regard this suggestion as the very suggestion of hell itself, and apply the other test.

But there is no need to argue this view merely on the theoretical plane. Let us apply the practical test. Read the Bible and study the story of its characters. Read the biographies of the greatest benefactors the world has ever seen. Read them especially in the light of what we have been discussing. Was David the King of Israel at his best and highest, was he expressing his true self when he applied the single test of pleasure in the matter of Bathsheba, thereby becoming a thief and a murderer? Was St. Augustine giving the truer expression to self when he was an immoral philosopher, or rather afterwards, when he became the disciplined saint who metaphorically cut off hands and feet, and plucked out eyes, the eyes of lust and evil desire? Think of all the members of the noble army of saints and martyrs who have denied themselves, disciplined their lives, curbed and controlled their impulses and instincts, and, in general, obeyed the teaching of the gospel! Compare and contrast them with the sensuous roués and libertines of history. Which of these two groups represents self, real human nature, most truly? It is insulting even to ask the question. The way to express self truly is the way of discipline and order, the way of reason and prayer, the way of hearkening to the voice of conscience and encouraging every uplifting thought and desire. The world may regard you as a fool, and from its standpoint you will certainly be halt and maimed and have but one eye. Yea, as an animal you may appear to be most imperfect. But you will be a man worthy of the name. You will have a self that will be worthy of expression, and which will grow from day to day. "Man shall not live by bread alone";[1] no, nor by pleasure alone. To live, his whole being and nature must be used and exercised. Otherwise he will die.

The case against this modern teaching is not yet complete. The fact that it ignores recklessly the ultimate destiny of this self of ours must also be mentioned. That it does so from a merely earthly and human standpoint has been made plain. But there is a higher standpoint, and an infinitely more important one, which it also entirely ignores. Our Lord said, "It is better for thee to enter into life halt or maimed, rather

[1] Luke iv. 4.

than having two hands or two feet to be cast into everlasting fire." Again, "It is better for thee to enter into life with one eye, rather than having two eyes to be cast into hell fire." Those are the words uttered by Jesus of Nazareth, the Son of God. On the purely human plane we have seen that this talk of self-expression is utterly degrading to the true self. But, over and above that, there is God's view of us, which is of infinitely greater consequence, as we are in His hands and He is the Judge eternal. That it is His view of self that matters is made abundantly clear in the Bible. Indeed, to teach that is the whole purpose of the Bible. God gave man a nature and a being like His own. He created man in His own image. He breathed into man the breath of life and made of him a living soul. That soul is God's gift to us. It is the treasure which He has committed to our charge and keeping. It is the self that He asks us to express and expects us to express. And at the end of life and of time He will test our performance. The standard of judgment will be the moral law as given to Moses, the teachings of the prophets, the Sermon on the Mount, and, above all, our believing knowledge of Himself and our approximation to the life lived by our Lord and Saviour, Jesus Christ. For true self-expression has been revealed perfectly once and for all in Him. The question we shall all have to face therefore is, What have you made of the self? How have you expressed it? The consequences are eternal—life or death, heaven or hell.

Before we begin, therefore, to talk about freedom for self-expression we must discover whether or not we have that true self which God has desired for all men. If we lack it, we cannot express it, and we shall not be able to hand it back to Him and give an account of it at the dread Day of Judgment. The one urgent question therefore confronting every man is the question, What of your self? Do you possess your soul? Is the true self still in existence? Are the vision and the divine faculty still there? Is your soul still alive? If you have lived only according to your instincts, desires, and impulses, the true self is long since dead, as you can easily discover if you but try to live the other life, and, above all, if you try to find God. Man cannot rehabilitate his true self. He cannot find God. Man can lose his own soul, but he can never find it again. He can kill and destroy it but he cannot create it anew. And were it not for one thing he would go inevitably to the eternal fire of hell. But, thank God, there is that one thing. "The Son of man is come to seek and to save that which was lost."[1] Jesus of Nazareth,

[1] Luke xix. 10.

the Son of God, came down to earth and lived and died and rose again in order to save. He has borne the punishment that we deserve on account of sin and for spoiling and marring the image of God upon us. But more, He restores our soul to us. He gives us a new nature and fills us with power that will enable us to express this new and true self even as He expressed it Himself. This self-expression expresses man as a son of God, well-pleasing in the sight of his Heavenly Father, and as an heir to eternal life. The world reduces man to the level of the beast, offends the holy Judge and leads to eternal death. The Bible, therefore, calls upon us to give up the pleasures of sin for a season and to find our true selves in Jesus Christ. It calls upon us to this end to deny ourselves, to cut off hand or foot, to pluck out eye, to do anything that may be necessary in order to serve the best and the highest interests of this true self, for it tells us that "it is better ... to enter into life halt or maimed, rather than having two hands or two feet to be cast into everlasting fire."

CHAPTER TWO

WHAT IS WRONG WITH MAN?

NEXT IN IMPORTANCE AND IN LOGICAL SEQUENCE TO the question, "What is man?" comes the vital question as to what is wrong with man. We can no more act on assumptions here than we could with the previous question as to man's real nature. The temptation, always, in a time of crisis and of trouble, is to rush into action and to apply various types of treatment. But intelligent treatment must always be preceded by diagnosis. There is, of necessity, an inevitable, logical connection between diagnosis and treatment. The one clearly determines the other and controls it. If we feel that there is but little wrong, our treatment will not be drastic. If, on the other hand, we take a serious view of the situation, then something more radical will be called for by way of treatment. Now, as we come to discuss this question as to what is wrong with man, we find, once more, that there are only two views, the Biblical and the non-Biblical. More than that, we find that these two positions are still exactly and precisely what they have always been, though the terminology may have changed somewhat. It is the same great contrast drawn in the Bible between what are called the true prophets and the false prophets; and all we have to say about the utterly false view, to-day, of what is wrong with man was said perfectly hundreds of years ago by the prophet Jeremiah, when he said of his contemporary false prophets, "They have healed also the hurt of the daughter of my people slightly, saying, Peace, peace; when there is no peace."[1] That type of false prophet is still with us; we still must face this question of what exactly is wrong with man.

As we look at the contemporary position in the light of the teaching of the Bible, we are reminded increasingly of the truth of Hegel's dictum that "history teaches us that history teaches us nothing." In spite of all we have experienced in the present century, with its two devastating wars, mankind still seems to harbour the same ancient illusions and is still guilty of fatal optimism with respect to man. Mankind indeed seems to be a kind of incorrigible Mr. Micawber, ever waiting for something to turn up, and ever confident that the solution to all our problems is awaiting us around some magical corner. The result is that the false prophet who prophesies ease and pleasure for us is as popular with us to-day as he was in Israel of old, and the true prophet is as much in disfavour as was

[1] Jer. vi. 14.

Jeremiah. The false prophets were optimistic. Jeremiah seemed to be an utter pessimist. But subsequent events proved him to be right. As our whole contention is that the very state of the modern world proves that the diagnosis of man's ills as it is to be found in the Bible is the only true and accurate one, we can do nothing better than consider the views of the Bible with respect to man's troubles in terms of that charge which Jeremiah brought against the false prophets of his age. It is a perfect analysis and condemnation of all the false optimism that is so popular at the present time.

Let us first of all, then, consider and expose the errors and the fallacies that underlie that optimistic view of life held by the false prophets who are ever ready to cry, "Peace, peace," and who assure us that all will soon be well. For one thing, it is clearly a superficial view of life, as is evident in the jauntiness with which such a view always expresses itself. With a smile on their faces, the false prophets always give the impression that the situation is quite simple and that they can deal with it readily. Indeed, the one thing that ever seems to perplex them is the fact that anyone should imagine for a moment that the situation is in any way difficult. This shallow optimism shows, of

34

course, a definite type of mentality; to whatever realm the problem may belong, its attitude is always the same. Take an illustration from the pseudo-scientific realm. You read the advertisement on a bottle of quack medicine, and you are given the impression that your malady can easily be cured. All you have to do is to take the remedy, and immediately all will be well. The confident assurances may give you the impression that the main trouble with the medical profession is that it magnifies problems and exaggerates difficulties. Or, to take another example, there was a manifestation of the self-same attitude and spirit during the last war. Recall the agitation for the opening of a second front in Europe. According to the writings and speeches of most of the amateur strategists, there was really no difficulty in the matter whatsoever. We had simply to cross the English Channel and to land an army in France and all would have been well. To these pundits there were no difficulties and no problems, and the impression was given that those who were ultimately responsible for strategy, namely, the highest military officials amongst the allies, were just dull and stupid. They were men who imagined difficulties and problems. To the others the whole situation seemed simple and clear. Now, it is precisely the same with respect to the whole problem of life and living. To the false prophet there is no real difficulty. His view of the situation is superficial. As Jeremiah said, he has healed or treated the hurt of the people "slightly" or lightly. His diagnosis is that there is but little wrong.

It is important that we should work this theory out in detail. The essence of the position is that man himself is all right fundamentally, and that his troubles, whatever they may be, do not spring from anything radically wrong in his own nature. To some of these theorists the problem of life and mankind and the world is simply one of development and evolution. Man, they argue, has developed and grown out of the animal, and it is inevitable that for a certain period of time he should still bear traces of the limits and imperfections imposed upon him by his animal nature. But the great thing to grasp, we are told, is that he is developing and progressing and improving. We are invited, therefore, to look back upon the story of man and to delight in observing the great progress that has been made. We are asked to compare man in his primitive, rude state with man as he is to-day. Then we are told by these authorities, with a most disarming, mock kind of modesty, that they are prepared to admit that man is not yet perfect, and that he still has a distance to travel. But the problem, they assure us, is purely one of time. We must be patient, and whatever may happen in our time and generation, we must realize that we are part of this great process that is ever certainly and surely working itself out in the direction of perfection. There is no need to be alarmed or disappointed over seeming discrepancies and reversions. Given time, everything will show itself to be all right. There is no need to elaborate this view, for it has been the most popular view concerning life for the past eighty to a hundred years.

Closely allied to that view is the one that regards the problems of man's life purely in terms of intellect and education. This view is not quite so mechanical as the former and does not insist so firmly on the inevitability of progress. It considers the real source of trouble to be man's failure to think and to reason. Man, according to this view, is not really evil, he just refuses to think! He is afflicted with a kind of mental inertia, due largely to the fact that he has not realized the true nature of the wonderful propensities that lie within him. For so many æons has he been accustomed to living like an animal, responding to the various instincts and impulses of his animal nature, and allowing his fate to be determined by forces and factors outside himself, that he is slow to assert these higher powers that reside within him. In his greed, he desires something and proceeds to take it, only to be resisted by someone else who desires the same thing. And since each is governed by greed and passion, they begin to fight for it. The result is that they destroy each other, and neither has the coveted prize. If only they had the good sense to pause at the beginning, and to think, reason, negotiate, how much better it would be for both. And why should they not do so? They both have the necessary faculties. They have the brains. According to this view, which was essentially that of the late H. G. Wells, there is no need to paint that dark and sombre picture of man in terms of sin and radical evil. Man's troubles are due simply to his stupidity and his refusal to think, and they can be cured by education.

Another common manifestation of this superficial view of the ills of mankind is seen in the statement that our troubles are due entirely and solely to conditions and surroundings. This, again, needs no elaboration, since we have been told constantly for many years that our troubles are due entirely to economic and social causes such as manifest themselves in terms of distribution of wealth and housing conditions. If anyone is disposed to suggest that I am caricaturing the position, and ridiculing it, I would simply ask such a person to listen to a man like J. B. Priestley as he jauntily solves all our problems in his broadcast talks, or to listen to the conversation of average men as they discuss these matters together. The impression always given is that the matter is quite simple. This impression of superficiality is given by the manner and the tone of voice as well as by the statements made with respect to the exact causes of our ills and troubles.

In exactly the same way, of course, a similar charge can be brought against the proposed treatment. Here again what is impressed upon us is the extreme ease with which all can be put right. There is no need for desperate remedies or radical cures. Above all, no need of a change in individual persons so radical as to merit the description of being born again or regenerated. All we need is to be educated, to think and plan, to organize and introduce certain measures of legislation which will equalize economic conditions, provide work for all, guarantee to everyone good housing conditions, and insure equality of opportunity for all. These are the modern counterparts of what was once expressed as "liberty, equality and fraternity," and in still earlier days, by the words, "peace, peace." The whole system is so simple. There is but little wrong, and it can soon be put right.

But we must examine this position a little more closely and critically, and we must face the question which immediately suggests itself to us—namely, why it is that mankind takes such a superficial view of the problem and its cure. Why are we all so ready to listen to and applaud the false prophets who cry, "Peace, peace"? The answer to the question is also supplied by the statement of Jeremiah. It is that the minds of the false prophets are so biased and prejudiced, and so controlled by certain ideas, as to make them incapable of true and clear thinking. This shows itself in two main ways.

We see it, first of all, in their general attitude, in their very approach to the problem. We have referred already to the jauntiness of spirit and of manner that ever characterizes such people. They give the impression from the very outset that they are determined not to find much wrong. We hear much these days about wishful thinking, and, whatever we may think of what has been called the new psychology, we all must agree that we tend to be controlled by prejudices, and that nothing is so difficult as to think freely and with an open mind. Some men by nature tend to minimize problems and difficulties, and others, equally by nature, tend to magnify them and exaggerate them. When two such men are called in to face precisely the same problem one can more or less predict what each is going to say. The confirmed optimist is certain to say, "It's all right," before he has even begun to

40

examine the problem. He is so anxious to find little wrong, and so ready to shout, "Peace, peace," that he is most unlikely to find much wrong. It is not that he is dishonest or that he refuses to see evidence, symptoms and signs. He is blinded by his prejudice.

The effect of the prejudice is seen equally clearly in the attitude of the false prophet to the true prophet. How bitter the false prophets in the old days were to Jeremiah and to others! Our Lord Himself once cried out in anguish of heart, "O Jerusalem, Jerusalem, thou that killest the prophets, and stonest them which are sent unto thee."[1] They were never content with just disobeying. They were bitter and venomous. That they hated and persecuted the prophets of God again shows a mentality which is the very reverse of a calm, scientific outlook. Clear thinking is impossible in such a state. Men who with bitterness and scorn and cursing dismiss religion are simply proclaiming that they have never considered it, for the reason that they are incapable of true thought with respect to it, however expert and well qualified they may be in other respects. We must admit that this is something which is still manifesting itself at the present time. Men are seldom content merely to disagree with the Biblical teaching. They must ridicule it and curse it. They must make

[1] Matt. xxiii. 37.

fun of it and display feeling and passion with respect to it. They simply indicate their prejudice, though to do so is the very antithesis of calm and cool reasoning.

But as the false prophet reveals his prejudice in general in that way, we can show equally clearly that it affects the details of his thought processes also. Is it not clear, for instance, that he starts by setting up a false standard? He places happiness before health. His great desire is to be able to say that all is well. The one thing he desires is to be free from pain. This is something with which we can all sympathize. In any condition of abnormality or illness the one thing that tends to monopolize our attention is the pain and the suffering. For the time being we tend to be interested in nothing else. We simply desire relief from pain, anything to lessen our agony and suffering. That is the one request we make of the physician who comes to treat us. And that is quite legitimate. It is essential for the one charged with treating us to do all he can to relieve our suffering. But should the physician be concerned about nothing but the relief of pain he would be not only a false physician but a positive menace to the best interests of his patient. For what a sick man really needs is not the mere alleviation of pain, but the cure of the disease which is causing the pain. Drugs which relieve pain may at the same time mask symptoms which are designed to call attention to the diseased condition. It is a simple thing to give an injection of morphine, for instance, to ease the pain from which a patient is suffering. But the alleviation of suffering without earnest search for the cause of the pain would brand a physician as almost criminally superficial. The pain is a symptom of a disease, and it is designed by nature to enable the attendant to track down the essential cause of the trouble. Or, to use another illustration, man under the influence of alcohol may feel perfectly happy for the time being, but the question is, has he solved his problems? To place happiness before health, and to regard it as the supreme good, is to be guilty of a fundamental fallacy in the matter of standards.

Such unthinking procedure includes also the further fallacy of failing to see that ultimately happiness depends upon health, and is something that results from health. Any other type of happiness is negative and dependent only upon the absence of conditions that prevent happiness. However much we may strive to lessen our unhappiness, while there is disease there can be no true happiness. Nothing is so fallacious, therefore, and so fatal to true happiness, as to make of ease and happiness ends in and of themselves. When our Lord said, "Blessed are they which do hunger and

43

thirst after righteousness: for they shall be filled,"[1] He did not say that they would be happy who hungered and thirsted after happiness. The blessedness, the happiness, the joy is something which will result from our seeking righteousness and from our becoming righteous. It is a by-product, an end result. We are not to place blessedness or happiness in the supreme position. We are to seek righteousness, and, having found it, we shall then find ourselves to be happy and filled with blessedness.

But what ultimately accounts for the failure of the false prophet to think clearly is the fact that he is deliberately determined to defend himself and to think well of himself. Pride is the root cause of the trouble. The view of the false prophet starts with the postulate that whatever else may be the cause of the troubles of life it is not man himself. Do we not all know something of this assumption in our own lives and experiences? There is nothing which we dislike so much as criticism or the suggestion that we are wrong. How expert we are at explaining away what we do, and at rationalizing our sins! How difficult it is to see defects and blemishes in ourselves which we recognize at a distance in others! Now, the view of the false prophet with respect to a man and his problems is identical, only

[1] Matt. v. 6.

on a large scale. The initial assumption is that man himself is all right. Therefore, the cause of the trouble must be looked for, and found, elsewhere; and nothing can be admitted as fact which questions man's inherent integrity. It is for this reason that Biblical teaching about sin in the human heart as the cause of all ills is resented bitterly, and is, above all else, the aspect of the gospel and its teaching to which men object. In other words, the court is packed before the case comes up for trial. The judge and jury are already bribed and biased. The verdict is decided upon before any evidence has been called. Man himself must be exonerated, and is, of course, exonerated. Setting out with a fixed determination to avoid anything unpleasant or disconcerting to our self-esteem and pride, and desiring, above all else, ease and happiness, he finds little difficulty in this view of life and takes but little time in persuading himself that all is well, and in shouting, "Peace, peace."

But the vital question is, Is there peace? By asking that question and giving the answer, the same answer that was given so long ago by Jeremiah, we arrive at our third statement concerning this shallow view of life. It is proved by the test of facts and of history to be altogether false. The false prophets cry, "Peace,

peace," but there is no peace. When shall we learn the lesson that there is no abiding peace in this world and cease to hearken to the false prophets? That it is necessary at all to emphasize this point at such a time as this, when we have just emerged from a second devastating world war within a quarter of a century, is proof in and of itself of the blindness of this fatal optimism that afflicts mankind by nature. But because of our pur-blindness it is a point which must be emphasized and repeated endlessly if we are to be saved. Let us therefore face such questions as the following: How much longer have we to wait before this upward surge and trend in mankind is going to evolve into a state of final and complete perfection? Is there any hope for us, or is it merely something that we are to dream about as happening after the passage of many further æons of time? Is there any real evidence that there is any such advance at all? Again, we must consider whether the world is becoming happier, better, kinder; whether the problems of life are gradually diminishing in number and decreasing in perplexity; and whether man's inhumanity to man is less evident than it once was. And still the problems press for answer: Is there proof of the increase of positive virtue? And what of this idea that all we need is to apply our brain power and develop our intellect and increase our knowledge?

Are men of ability free from problems? Does intellect guarantee a life of perfect happiness? Is a man who has acquired knowledge and culture of necessity a paragon of all the virtues? Is such a man immune to all the diseases and trials to which flesh is heir? Does he invariably apply his knowledge and reasoning powers when he is attracted by that which he knows to be wrong or harmful, but which, nevertheless, appeals to him and which he enjoys? For the answers we have but to read the great literature of the world. Such men are sometimes among the greatest sufferers in the world, and they have often endured more poignant agonies of mind and of spirit than any other type. Indeed, in the realm of their personal relationships they often fail most tragically. The Baconian philosophy, "Knowledge is power," has become a popular modern slogan. But history, biography, the records of the courts of law, and the columns of the newspapers tell a very different story. Quite apart from all that, however, if our salvation lies in intellect and knowledge, what hope is there for those who are not gifted with great intellect, and who therefore cannot hope to learn? A salvation that can save only some is a mockery and a travesty of the word.

In precisely the same way we may see that a mere change of conditions cannot possibly solve the problem.

Are all who have sufficient wealth happy? Does the possession of things, houses, goods, really solve all problems? Which is the more likely to be happy, the rich man or the poor man, the dweller in the west end of a city or the inhabitant of the east end? In which class do the greater number of tragedies take place, or in which is the greater depth of misery and desolation experienced? The answer is, of course, that ultimately conditions make but little difference to our happiness and to the character of our life. At least, if they do we are living a most precarious and contingent type of life. The things that determine our type of life are much deeper—love or hatred, envy or generosity of spirit, selfishness or a disposition to help others, and all the various other qualities of character that go to determine human relationships. Our problems and troubles arise from ourselves and what we are. It is not that we deny the value of education or economic conditions. All men are entitled to a measure of decent living in this present world and should demand it as their right, but to say that it alone is necessary, and that they, alone, can solve our every problem, is to display an utterly false view of life. Indeed, we are reminded increasingly of those words of Shakespeare,

> The fault, dear Brutus, is not in our stars,
> But in ourselves, that we are underlings.

Those who cry, "Peace, peace," on such a superficial basis are false prophets to whom the facts of life reply vociferously, tragically, "There is no peace."

Before the problems of life and of man can be solved we must first of all realize the true nature of the problem. To that end we must shed our prejudices and cease to be governed by our desires. We must be prepared for honest thought, and a thoroughgoing examination and analysis, which will probe us to the very depths and search our motives as well as our actions. Where are such an examination and analysis to be found? It is of the very essence of the Christian religion to say that they are to be found alone in the Bible. There we have the revelation of what God thinks of man and what God has done about man. Its view is repeated and illustrated therein endlessly. According to this Book, man's troubles are due to the fact that he has sinned and rebelled against God. He was created in a state of happiness which depended upon his relationship to God and his obedience to God's laws and God's will. But man rebelled against God's will and therefore broke the law of his own nature. As we have seen, happiness follows health. Nowhere is this succession seen more than in the spiritual and moral realms. Man has become unhealthy.

A disease called sin has ravaged his being. Man refuses to recognize his corruption and resorts to the various expedients we have been considering in an attempt to find happiness and peace. But invariably he fails, for the trouble is not only within himself and in his surroundings, but also in his relationship to God. Man is fighting against the only One who can give him what he needs and desires. God has said, "There is no peace to the wicked."[1] Man, therefore, by fighting God, by resisting and disobeying Him, is robbing himself of the very prize that he covets. And whatever he may do, until a relationship of obedience to God is restored, he will never know health and happiness. He may multiply his wealth and possessions, he may perfect his educational facilities, he may gain the whole world of wealth and knowledge; but to do so will profit him nothing so long as his relationship to God is not right. There will always be something lacking, even in his greatest joy; he will never know true satisfaction. He will find fault with his circumstances and change them, but the relief will be only temporary. He will blame other people and form new associations and alliances, but soon he will be unhappy again. He will censure this and that, and resort to this expedient and the other, until, like Hamlet, finding

[1] Isa. lvii. 21.

all insufficient, he will cry out in bitterness, saying:

> The time is out of joint; O cursèd spite,
> That ever I was born to set it right!

He feels that he himself is all right, and that his troubles arise elsewhere. And on, and on, and on he will go in his misery and his wretchedness, and with his futile experiments, until, like the once profligate and sinful Augustine, he comes to realize that the trouble is within himself and in his wrong relationship to God, and cries out, "Thou hast created us for thyself and our hearts are restless until they find their rest in thee." But, coming to this realization, he will begin to feel that his case is utterly hopeless. He will see not only his folly but his arrogance. He will feel that he has forfeited every claim on the love of God. But, wonder of wonders, he hears the gospel which tells him that God, in spite of all his disobedience, has been patiently waiting for him. Indeed, he finds that God has been seeking him and has sent His Son, Jesus Christ, into the world to find him and to deliver him. He is told that Christ has already died for his guilt. He is assured of pardon and given a new life and a new nature. He now sees all things in a new way. Problems are solved and difficulties are banished. He begins to experience peace which is true peace, for it is not solely dependent upon others and outward conditions. Rather, it is a peace that persists in spite of changing conditions, a deep, inner quietness which he can describe only as "the peace of God, which passeth all understanding."[1] He has found that "being justified by faith, we have peace with God."[2] And, seeing himself and all others in this new light shed upon man and his world by the Bible and its teaching, he is also full of concord with others. There can be no peace among men until it is found within man, and that ideal can be obtained only by our surrendering ourselves to Him who said, "Peace I leave with you, my peace I give unto you: not as the world giveth, give I unto you. Let not your heart be troubled, neither let it be afraid."[3]

[1] Phil. iv. 7.   [2] Rom. v. 1.   [3] John xiv. 27.

CHAPTER THREE

SINCERITY *VERSUS* TRUTH

MORE AND MORE, WHEN ONE CONSIDERS AND EXAMINES the present position in the light of the Biblical teaching, one realizes that all the popular fallacies with respect to life and its troubles are but modern variants of very old ideas. We have already seen the truth of this statement as we have considered the problems of man's true nature and what is wrong with man. Now, as we proceed to consider what is to be done for him, we shall find once more that one of the most popular theories is one which is exposed and dealt with very clearly in the Bible.

There is nothing, perhaps, more moving in the Bible than the concern expressed by the Apostle Paul for his fellow countrymen, the Jews. He was grieved at their persistent and obstinate refusal to believe the gospel. He felt that because of their privileged position their case was more tragic than that of any other people. God had chosen them out of all nations, and had given to them special prerogatives. To them had been entrusted the Scriptures, and they had been trained by a wonderful succession of prophets to look forward to the coming of a great Messiah and Deliverer. Yet it was they, of all people, who had rejected Christ and who still refused to believe the gospel concerning Him. They who were looking forward to the coming of the Messiah did not recognize Him when He came. They who declared themselves anxious to be just with God were rejecting the one way whereby mankind can be justified before God. To Paul there was but one explanation of that tragedy. He expressed it in the words, "I bear them record that they have a zeal of God, but not according to knowledge."[1] He granted that the views were quite honest and quite sincere. The trouble with the Jews was not that they lacked sincerity, but rather that they trusted to it, and, because of their reliance on it, neglected to consider the further light and knowledge which the gospel could give them on the very object that they desired. Again, their difficulty was not that they lacked fervour but that they trusted to it, and argued that because they were zealous they were therefore of necessity right. "They have a zeal of God, but not according to knowledge." Indeed, they rejected the knowledge which the gospel was offering them because of that very ardour. The conflict in their case was between zeal and knowledge, between sincerity and truth.

[1] Rom. x. 2.

This particular theory must be considered because it happens to give an exact and precise description of the case of a large number of people at the present time. Indeed, one need not hesitate to say that it is a perfect description of the predominating tendency in much religious thought, a tendency which Paul called both pathetic and dangerous. It is the tendency to equate sincerity and truth, to put up zeal and knowledge as equivalent terms. It is not stated in exactly that way, of course, but rather thus, that if a man is sincere and zealous nothing else really matters. There can be no doubt at all but that these qualities, zeal and sincerity, are being exalted in our day precisely as they were by the Jews of old, and that they are the tests which are applied to all men and all ideas. Knowledge is being depreciated, almost despised. Clear, logical thinking and exact definitions are at a discount. Doctrine and dogma are taboo and regarded as being almost the enemies of truth, and even good deeds are not given the prominence that they had a few years ago. To-day sincerity is often the sole test that is applied. It alone counts, and if a man can be proved sincere in his views, nothing more is demanded. The rightness or wrongness of the view is not considered. Indeed, it is regarded as being an irrelevance. For anyone to ask a question about the truth of a statement is considered as almost a sacrilege, a sign of a legal, quarrelsome mind and spirit. The reply to all comments and queries is that the man is honest in his views. Sincerity is the supreme test; and what is demanded of all is not that they should hold the right view, but that they should hold some view sincerely. Thus one often hears a phrase like this at the end of a meeting. "Of course, I didn't agree with him, but that doesn't matter. He was obviously sincere."

This position has doubtless come about largely as a reaction to certain conditions which previously existed. It is the modern reaction against mere theology, mere knowledge, mere morality. The modern man hates cant and hypocrisy. He abominates that type of person, who was said to be so common toward the end of the last century, whose head was full of knowledge and of theology, but whose heart was devoid, not only of the grace of the Lord Jesus Christ, but also of the ordinary milk of human kindness. The modern man loathes that kind of individual whose morality is only skin deep, and whose religion seems to be confined to only one day in seven. He feels that there has been exhibited far too much of that kind of intellectual interest in religion and theology which fails to express itself in practice. "What we need," he says, "is sincerity. Let a man's view be what it may, only let it be sincere." Orthodoxy without honesty, morality without manliness, and superficial "saintliness" which lacks sincerity are to the modern man the greatest evils. What is needed above all else, he feels, is genuineness, sincerity, a passion for righteousness, whatever particular views one may hold on doctrine or theology.

There is much, of course, in all this with which we must all agree. Sincerity is essential; without it one cannot hope to arrive at truth. The insincere person cannot be defended. But to say that sincerity and truth are identical is to fall into an error which is quite as dangerous as to hold the truth insincerely. Sincerity is needed. It is essential. But when the contention is made, as it is being made, that really nothing matters but honesty and a zeal for truth, then the pendulum has swung right over to the other extreme, which is quite as dangerous as that of which those living at the end of the last century were said to be guilty.

Let us, then, consider this modern position in detail, and especially in the light of what Paul says about his own contemporaries who in terms of zeal and sincerity rejected the gospel of Jesus Christ. Consider, first of all, the fallacy which is involved in this modern tendency to place zeal in the position of knowledge, and to exalt sincerity to the place of truth. When I say fallacy I mean, primarily, an intellectual and philosophical fallacy. Apart from its error in the particular sphere of religion, it is faulty and foolish when considered in any sphere, or in any particular application.

For one thing, it indicates failure on the part of such people to realize the true meaning and nature of zeal and sincerity. What, after all, is zeal? What do earnestness and sincerity stand for? Surely they are nothing more, and are meant to convey nothing more, than a description of the way in which one performs a particular action or travels towards a given destination. They announce that the man's way of travelling is wholehearted and thorough, that there is no suspicion of lethargy or dishonesty about his method. He is clearly anxious to arrive at his desired goal, and he strains every nerve and muscle in order to get there. Such are zeal, honesty, and sincerity. Or, to take another illustration, one may preach the gospel sincerely or insincerely. Or one may advocate a political or a social cause genuinely and honestly, or because of some personal interest or some ulterior motive. It is but a description of the way in which one performs or carries out any function; it is not concerned with the function as an end in itself. Surely one's object in setting out on a journey is not merely to travel in a particular manner. One is not content until one arrives

58

at the destination. But the idea of a goal is precisely what is being forgotten to-day. All the emphasis is on the zeal and the sincerity; the way in which one journeys is regarded as being of greater importance than the destination. Travelling has become an object in itself. Let me cite but one typical and well-known instance of this. In writing about the quest for truth, Rufus M. Jones says definitely and distinctly that if he were offered in one hand the thrill and the joy of the quest for truth, and in the other truth itself, he would without the slightest hesitation choose the former. Now, that is typical of much of the modern view. The whole emphasis is on the quest, and on the way in which one searches. Seeking has become more important than finding. Thus sincerity and zeal are exalted above all else. Travelling in itself has become the object of desire. The goal is regarded as being unimportant, indeed almost an annoyance; for arriving at the goal of necessity means the end of this delightful and exhilarating quest. What a terrible perversion of thought, to say nothing of religion. The Jesuits of old were condemned because they taught that the end justifies the means. But to-day the idea is that the means alone matter and that the end does not count at all. It matters not what our ultimate view and idea may be, so long as we are sincere.

But I can imagine someone putting forward the objection that this is not quite fair, that the modern case is really not that sincerity and zeal are in and of themselves the object of worship, but that, rather, the case is that sincerity is a guarantee of truth, that any view held quite sincerely must therefore be right. The argument is that if we seek for truth and reality sincerely, our very sincerity is a guarantee that we shall ultimately arrive at our goal. But this leaves the position exactly where it was before; for the error here is quite as great. It is the error of thinking and imagining that it is one of the functions of zeal and sincerity to decide as to the rightness or wrongness of the ultimate goal, and of the direction in which we are travelling. But as we have already seen, that is not their function at all. Their business is to help us to arrive at that goal. Sincerity and zeal are to men what petrol is to the motor car, what steam is to the engine. They are but expressions of power, and are therefore in no way competent to decide or to determine the right or wrong turns along the road. But that is exactly how they are being used at the present time. "Do you see that man?" people say. "He is all out for the truth. He leaves no stone unturned. He does all he can. Notice his amazing zeal and sincerity." He is all out, and, because he is thus all out, it is taken for granted that he must be right and that he must in no sense be criticized. Now, this attitude is as fallacious as for one to say that because we are travelling very quickly along a certain road, and because the throttle of the automobile is all out, that therefore we must of necessity be on the right road. No! The rate and speed and method of travelling are no guarantee at all that we are on the right road. It is not within the competence of sincerity and zeal to determine the rightness or the wrongness of the view which we hold.

But this point is seen still more clearly when we realize that zeal and sincerity can be right or wrong and still remain zeal and sincerity. In other words, we must remind ourselves that one can be sincerely wrong and quite genuinely mistaken. Perhaps the classic instance of this is the case of St. Paul himself. He tells us repeatedly that in the days before his conversion, when he persecuted the church of God, and massacred Christians, and did his utmost to exterminate the Christian cause, he was perfectly sincere. He did it "in all good conscience."[1] He not only thought that he was right, he was certain that he was right; and he believed from the depths of his being that he was doing that which was well-pleasing in God's sight. He was sincere and zealous. He was all out. There was

[1] Acts xxiii. 1.

no trace of hypocrisy or of sham in his action. If ever there was an honest man it was Saul of Tarsus before his conversion. But on the way to Damascus he suddenly came to see that he had been terribly and tragically wrong. He saw that his whole direction had been wrong, and he immediately turned right about. Afterwards he worked and travelled with equal enthusiasm in exactly the opposite direction. The sincerity and the zeal remained precisely the same, but the direction that was given to them was entirely different. Before his conversion Paul was sincerely wrong. After his conversion he was sincerely right. That a man is sincere is, therefore, no guarantee of rightness, and to make it the standard and the ultimate test is just to throw logic and clear thinking to the winds. And, surely, we must admit that many of the greatest cruelties and excesses recorded in ancient, and, indeed, in modern, history must be attributed to a false sincerity and to a zeal that was not governed and controlled by knowledge.

In other words, and in order to end this pure bit of argumentation, what seems to have been forgotten is that we can say of sincerity what is said of fire in the well-known adage: "Fire is a good servant but a bad master." So long as it is under control, nothing is more valuable than fire. We can heat our rooms with it, cook our meals, and perform an endless number of beneficial actions with it. But once fire ceases to be under control and itself becomes the master, it leads to nothing but destruction and havoc. Or we may take the illustration of a well-bred, powerful, spirited horse. Nothing is more enjoyable than to be seated on such a horse as long as one is firmly in the saddle, and has a solid grip on the reins. But should such a horse take the bit between his teeth and bolt, the position would become precarious and the incident end in disaster. Now, the case is precisely the same with sincerity. Given knowledge in the saddle, given knowledge and truth in control, nothing is finer or more important than sincerity. But if we hand over the control to sincerity itself it may well lead us hopelessly astray and land us in disaster. That is what had happened to St. Paul before his conversion. That was the trouble, he tells us, with the Jews of his own day. They had sincerity, but not according to knowledge. It was not being directed. It was a sincerity without sight or vision; it was causing destruction and leading to damnation. Given knowledge and right direction, there is nothing that is so essential as sincerity. But when one relies upon the pressure of steam in the engine rather than on the compass for the right direction there can be but one result, shipwreck. At the present time masses of people are steaming ahead in this supposedly great quest for truth and reality. They protest that they are sincere and genuine, that they are "all out for truth"; but in the name of God we ask them, "Where are you going? Have you the knowledge? Is your compass working? Are you still keeping your eye on the north star? Do you not think it is time for you to take your bearing and to discover your exact position? Are you not aware of certain grave dangers which are liable to meet you at any moment in this voyage and in this quest? Stop for a moment. Realize the danger of trusting only to power. Realize the all-importance of knowledge and truth, of information and direction." There is surely nothing which is quite so foolish, and quite so false, as to trust only to a sincerity and a zeal which are not directed by knowledge.

But let us consider also the futility of this position. Let us consider what a terrible waste of energy is involved when sincerity and zeal are undirected by knowledge and truth. The situation exists, of course, in every realm. For instance, if we are concerned about scientific experimentation, to trust only to keenness and sincerity in the quest for results without having a certain amount of knowledge is clearly useless and may be highly dangerous. In any department of life knowledge is essential, and mere fervency apart from it cannot produce the desired result. Now, when we realize that we are concerned ultimately with God, and with pleasing Him, how infinitely more important it is to realize that knowledge of His will and His purpose with respect to us is absolutely vital before we proceed to any action whatever.

This truth is something which can be demonstrated in two main ways. Paul's argument with respect to the views of his contemporaries was, first of all, that trusting as they did to their zeal and sincerity, apart from knowledge, they succeeded in doing nothing but establishing their own righteousness. The cause of their error, he says, was that they were ignorant of God's righteousness; that they were ignorant not only of God's way of salvation, but of what God really demands. Our Lord Himself once brought precisely the same charge against the Pharisees when He said, "Ye are they which justify yourselves before men; but God knoweth your hearts: for that which is highly esteemed among men is abomination in the sight of God."[1] Could anything be quite so futile and so useless as this state of affairs? It is perhaps to be seen most clearly in the case of the Jews in the time of our Lord

[1] Luke xvi. 15.

and Paul. There they were with all their zeal and sincerity, their good works and their morality. They denied themselves and suffered; they prayed and fasted and gave of their goods to feed the poor. And yet their mighty works were all of no value, for the simple reason that they were not what God asked of them. They had set up their own standards. They were working according to their own ideas and traditions, and, having done all, they were able to point to great achievements and to a huge mass of righteousness which they had worked up in this manner. But it was all worthless. It was only their own righteousness, and not the righteousness which God demanded: and what made the matter still more ridiculous was that they had persuaded themselves that it was all for God. They set out, they said, to please God and to justify themselves before Him, yet at the end all they had done was to please themselves. All because they would not listen to what God Himself had said. All because they trusted to their own zeal, and to their own ideas, and refused to be enlightened as to what God really demanded.

Now consider. Are there not those who do the same thing to-day? Those who ignore God's word; who refuse to consider the gospel, with its light and its knowledge; who keep away from God's house and every form of instruction with respect to these matters; who argue that all that is necessary is that one should be sincere, that one should pay one's twenty shillings in the pound, give to charity, be friendly and affable? To them we must say what Paul said to his contemporaries, that having done all, they are simply establishing their own righteousness. We are not questioning their sincerity or their honesty. We grant them both, as Paul did the Pharisees of old. But the vital question is, What is the value of it all? It is not God's way. It is not God's idea of righteousness, but simply their own. Surely the essence of wisdom is that before we begin to act at all, or to attempt to please God, we should discover what it is that God has to say about the matter. We must first learn His idea of righteousness, His demands. But the men and women of to-day, like the Jews of old, take their orders everywhere except from God's word. They rely upon the statements of certain modern writers, and live lives according to their own ideas rather than according to the teachings of Jesus of Nazareth, the Son of God. But let them go on. Let them continue blindly and ignorantly in their own way. Let them establish their own righteousness and refuse the gospel of Jesus Christ, and the day will surely come when they will discover that "that which is highly esteemed among men is

67

abomination in the sight of God."[1] The vital question to ask, therefore, is, Whom are we really pleasing? Is it ourselves or God? Have we yielded to His way? Can we say that we have submitted our wills and surrendered them to Him? If we have not, all our righteousness is "as filthy rags"[2] and will avail us nothing.

The second way in which we can demonstrate the futility of thus trusting to zeal at the expense of knowledge is to remind ourselves of the standard which is set for us by God. Paul reminded his contemporaries that Moses in giving the law to the Jews had said, "The man which doeth those things shall live by them."[3] That may be translated thus: "Anyone who can perform it shall live by it." God had given His law, His view of righteousness, and had said, in effect, "If you keep all that, you will have followed my commandments. That is what I demand. That is the only way of pleasing me." What is that way? Look at it. Consider it deeply. We talk about pleasing God by our own sincere efforts. Well, consider what we should have to do. Can man atone for his own past sins and misdeeds? Can he blot out his own transgressions? Can he sharpen his conscience and cleanse his memory? More than these, can he live in the present in a manner that truly satisfies himself? Can he with-

[1] Luke xvi. 15.   [2] Isa. lxiv. 6.   [3] Rom. x. 5.

68

stand temptation? Does he always live up to his own standard? Can he control his thoughts, his desires, inclinations, and imaginations as well as his every action? In other words, by his very greatest efforts can he, and does he, succeed in really living up to his own standard of life? Then consider God's standard. Read the law as given to the children of Israel, the Ten Commandments and the moral law which St. Paul, with all his zeal, could not keep when once he saw their true meaning. Then read the Sermon on the Mount and our Lord's various statements about the holiness of God. Then ponder His own perfect life. That is what we have to do. That is the righteousness which we should have to attain. Can any man do it? Can all the good intentions, and all the sincerity, and all the zeal of which anyone is capable, ever provide sufficient power to scale such heights? That is the mount which we should have to climb—the mount of the holiness of God. We are told that without holiness no man shall see the Lord.[1] Is there anyone who is capable of producing such holiness? Is the power in the little engine of our life sufficient to take us to such a height? Ask St. Paul. Ask Augustine, Luther, John Wesley. Ask all the noblest souls that the world has ever seen, all the sincerest and most

[1] Heb. xii. 14.

zealous spirits that mankind has ever produced. And as one mighty chorus, and with one accord, they answer saying,

> Not the labours of my hands
> Can fulfil Thy law's demands.
> Could my zeal no respite know,
> Could my tears for ever flow,
> All for sin could not atone.

And if they have failed, who are we to succeed? Oh, the folly and futility, the blindness and conceit of it all. Our best, our all is not enough. And let us point out that if this is the case with the sincere and the zealous, how much more hopelessly doomed to failure are those who make no effort at all, or who go on thoughtlessly and heedlessly living in sin, and who are really not concerned about God at all!

But consider, finally, the tragedy of this position. The tragedy lies in the fact that all this misery is unnecessary in view of the knowledge which is available. What made the Apostle Paul feel this so keenly, no doubt, was the fact that he had experienced it all himself, as he tells us in so many places in his writings and sermons. He had known what it was to trust to his own zeal and sincerity, and to his own efforts. He knew all about the striving and the sweating, the fasting and all the mighty efforts. But he knew also the feeling of hopelessness. He knew the failure to find satisfaction. And then he had experienced that glorious release which had come to him with the knowledge of the gospel. But here were his fellow countrymen still going on in the old way, still guilty of the old fallacy, still striving to do the impossible. He looked at them and saw their zeal and their great effort. "How sad," he cried, "how tragic! They have the zeal and the sincerity, but it is of no value. They are trying to justify themselves, but they never can; and while they are thus trying and failing they are deliberately refusing the knowledge which could give them in reality everything they desire and more." It was bad enough that all that energy and effort should be a sheer waste; but the tragedy was heightened and made infinitely greater by the contemplation of what they might have been if they had but accepted the gospel. They not only failed, but they utterly refused to be made successful. They preferred to trust to themselves and their own zeal and their own efforts and fail, rather than trust themselves to Jesus Christ and be saved. They were so anxious to do things themselves that they refused God's offer of eternal salvation as a pure gift. It was available, and being offered by the Apostles and others in the preaching of the gospel that

"Christ is the end of the law for righteousness to every-one that believeth."[1] They had but to believe that Jesus of Nazareth was the Son of God, that He had died to atone for their sins, and had risen again from the grave in order to justify them, and they would find themselves righteous in the sight of God and receive forgiveness of their sins. They said they wanted to be right with God; yet they deliberately refused the one way of being put right with God.

But what of the modern man? Is he not in a like position? Is he not trusting for salvation to himself, his own sincerity and his own efforts? Why is it that he still refuses the gospel concerning Jesus Christ and His atoning death and glorious Resurrection? Think again of the utter folly and futility of that position. Contemplate once more the task which faces us, and what is demanded of us. It is all utterly impossible for man in his own effort. Try to think of being in the presence of God; and if you realize to any extent what that means you will be compelled to agree with him who said,

> Eternal light! eternal light!
> How pure the soul must be,
> When, placed within thy searching sight,
> It shrinks not, but with calm delight
> Can live and look on thee!

[1] Rom. x. 4.

> Oh, how shall I, whose native sphere
> Is dark, whose mind is dim,
> Before the Ineffable appear,
> And on my naked spirit bear
> That uncreated beam?

How can one rise to perfect purity? How can all our zeal and sincerity get us there? The one way is outlined in the third stanza:

> There is a way for man to rise
> To that sublime abode:
> An offering and a sacrifice,
> A Holy Spirit's energies,
> An advocate with God.

The Son of God came to die for us and for our sins. He now offers to clothe us with His righteousness, and to present us faultless before God in eternity. There is no need for us to exhaust ourselves further in futile efforts. There is no need for heroics and the much-lauded quest for God. We have but to lay our sins on Jesus, for He is the propitiation for our sins and for the sins of the whole world.[1] Our all is not enough. But He is all sufficient. Zeal and sincerity, without knowledge which comes alone through Him, are vain and futile. But "if thou shalt confess with thy mouth the Lord Jesus, and shalt believe in thine heart that God hath raised Him from the dead, thou shalt be saved."[2]

[1] I John ii. 2.   [2] Rom. x. 9.

73

CHAPTER FOUR

THE SIMPLE GOSPEL

WE TURN NOW TO A MORE DIRECT AND POSITIVE consideration of what the gospel of Jesus Christ has to say about man, his ills and troubles, their treatment and their cure. As we do so, we are impressed at the very outset by the fact that the gospel, in complete and entire contrast to all rival ideas and theories, is characterized above all else by an essential simplicity and directness. I would not be understood as saying that the gospel is simple in the sense that I or anyone else can understand it, or grasp it fully with the mind, but, rather, that it is essentially simple in its view of life and in the way in which it deals with life. As regards the gospel itself, and all it means and implies, we have nothing to do but to acknowledge our feebleness and our nothingness, and to cry out with St. Paul, "Great is the mystery of godliness."[1] It is baffling in its immensity. Its very presuppositions transcend our highest categories of thought and of philosophy. We shall never fully understand the gospel itself to all eternity; but while we cannot claim that we can

[1] 1 Tim. iii. 16.

74

understand the gospel, or say that it itself is simple, we nevertheless can understand its view of life and grasp it: hence we may say that its main characteristics are simplicity and directness.

The distinction involved is vital. I would emphasize it for the reason that I believe there are large numbers of people outside the Church, and outside Christ, at the present time solely because they have not grasped that all-important distinction. They have confused understanding the working of the gospel with understanding the gospel itself. They seem to have determined not to allow the gospel to work on their lives until they understand the gospel itself. Their reason for this course, they say, is that they do not desire to commit intellectual suicide and to submit themselves passively to what they do not understand. The fear of passivity is a genuine and a good one, for there are many kinds of powers about us which are ready to possess us; and it is generally the uncritical, those who refuse to think and who will not discriminate, who ever become the first victims of the latest craze or cult. The gospel places no premium on our ignorance. Indeed, it teaches us that we must use the mind and the powers with which God has endowed us. But when it is suggested that by submitting ourselves to the gospel, and by allowing it to influence our lives, we are committing intellectual suicide simply because we cannot understand the gospel itself, then it seems clear that we are guilty of a fallacy and are behaving in an unreasonable and irrational manner. Let me illustrate. It is clear, is it not, that we know much more about light and heat than we know about the sun itself? In other words, we understand a great deal about the functions and the working of the sun while the sun itself in its essential nature and constitution remains a mystery to us. Or take electricity as an example. Here, again, we know a great deal more about its use than we do about the nature of electricity itself. There is nothing unreasonable about availing ourselves of the benefit offered by electricity even though we do not understand the thing itself, for we are not passive in our use of it. There are many tests which we can apply, and there are many laws which have been discovered and worked out concerning it and its use. We may know a great deal about these laws without understanding the essential nature of electricity itself. We are saved, for instance, from the danger of putting our hand on a live current by this knowledge. Although we cannot grasp what is meant when we are told that "the electron moves in its orbit around the proton in the atom a quadrillion times a second," we can nevertheless understand a good deal about the working of electricity and, up to a point, we can test and measure it with accuracy.

In the religious and the theological realm it is much the same. The mystery of godliness remains a mystery, and will ever remain so. The thing itself, as it was conceived and planned in the mind of God, is inscrutable and infinite; and as we contemplate it our minds are baffled. But that is not the case with regard to the effects and the results and the working out of the gospel. Here we can apply a number of tests. We can compare the Old Testament and the New Testament. We can compare scripture with scripture, and we have expert manuals of instruction written by the Apostles and others, and afterwards expounded by the saints and fathers, none of whom can be charged with lack of intellectuality. It is then in regard to the gospel view of life, and its proffered remedy for the ills of life, that we can say that the gospel is characterized above all else, and in contradistinction to all other ideas, by this essential directness and simplicity. And this is the explanation of the apparent paradox whereby it comes to pass that the gospel, on the one hand, has ever baffled, and is still baffling, the greatest philosophers the world has ever known, and yet can save a little child.

Another seemingly strange contradiction is the fact

that men and women, instead of glorying in the simplicity of the gospel, and rejoicing in it, have almost invariably objected to it. This point of view has been dominant not only outside the Church but often inside also. One has but to compare the Roman Catholic Church with the Church of the New Testament to see this contradiction clearly. The tendency always is to make religion involved and complex; and this tendency is very marked at the present time. As life in general becomes more and more complex, so religion tends to be affected in the same way. In the secular world, life to-day has become involved and sophisticated; in every direction one sees increased organization and multiplicity of machinery. Bustle and business, conferences and conventions are the order of the day. Never has the life of the world been so complicated. The excuse given is that the problems are so great! Principles have been forgotten. The simple truths are being ignored, and men spend their time in holding conferences to explore their difficulties. The same tendency is seen in the world of religion. It seems to be assumed that if the affairs of men are so difficult and complicated, the affairs of God should be still more complicated, because they are still greater. Hence comes the tendency to increase ceremony and ritual, and to multiply organizations and activities,

78

fellowships and institutions. The argument is still the same—namely, that as the problems and difficulties of life increase, so the Church must enlarge her organization and her methods. Put in a phrase, the argument is that it is ridiculous to assert that the vast problems of life to-day can be solved in the apparently simple manner suggested by those who preach the gospel in the old evangelical manner.

Now to this charge there are two main replies. The first is that it is always a very dangerous thing to argue from man to God, and to assume that what is true of man is always true of God, but in a still greater measure. For the Bible suggests that whereas this conclusion was apparently true, up to a point, at the beginning, it all became changed by the entry of sin into the world. Until man sinned, life was simple. The effect of sin from the very beginning was to create complications and difficulties. How perfectly is this fact illustrated in the first chapter of the book of Genesis. Look at it in the case of Adam and Eve. See it still more clearly marked in the case of Cain, who was the first to build a city. See it later in the attempt to erect the tower of Babel. Indeed it is shown everywhere. The fact is, that as we get further away from God life becomes more complicated and involved. We see this not only in the Bible, but also in subsequent history. The Protestant reformation simplified not only religion, but the whole of life and living in general, as did also the Puritan era and the evangelical awakening of the eighteenth century. The truly religious life is always simple.

Indeed, it is possible to go further and say with reverence that there is nothing which is so characteristic of God's work in every realm as its essential simplicity and order. Look where you will, you see that God ever works on an uncomplicated design. See how He repeats the seasons year by year—spring, summer, autumn, winter. Examine a flower, dissect an animal, and you will find that the basic pattern of nature is always simple. Simplicity is God's method. Is it, then, reasonable to believe that in the most vital subject of all, the salvation of man and the ordering of his life, God should suddenly jettison His own method and become involved and complex? To suggest that is to suggest a contradiction in the mind of God Himself.

But one has more than a shrewd suspicion, at times, that the objection to the directness and simplicity of the gospel is not so purely intellectual as it would have one believe. The real objection is to be found elsewhere. There is nothing which is quite so convenient and comforting as a sense of vagueness in connection with religion. As long as it is kept nebulous and indefinite, and as long as its followers can be busy with various activities, they can persuade themselves that all is well with them. In the absence of clear, precise definitions no discomfort is caused. The more complicated the religion, the more accommodating and comfortable does it prove. There is nothing which is so disconcerting as a plain, direct gospel which, stripping away all mere decorations and embellishments, and ignoring all non-essentials and make-believes, exposes the naked soul and flashes on to it the light of God. How much easier it is to appreciate the ceremony and ritual, to indulge in high-sounding, idealistic generalities, and to be busy with philanthropic actions—how much more gratifying to the natural self are these than to face the simple direct questions of the Word of God. Idealists and humanists are rarely, if ever, persecuted.

But leaving all that, let us proceed to consider positively the gospel view of life, and the solution of the gospel for the problems of life. That there is nothing which is so characteristic of it as its essential simplicity, is seen most clearly perhaps if we look at it in the light of some words that were spoken by the Lord Jesus Christ. He said, "The light of the body is the eye: therefore when thine eye is single, thy whole body also is full of light; but when thine eye is evil, thy body also is full of darkness."[1] If we work out the picture that is found in those words, we shall be able to see plainly the simplicity of the gospel. Our Lord says that what the eye is to the body in the matter of light, so the soul is to man, and so the individual man is to society. Thus we see that there is in man something which is vital and central. Man is not a mere collection and aggregate of parts. There is a centre to his life called the soul, as vital to his life as the eye is to the body in the matter of light. We see therefore that the gospel holds no mechanistic view of man. There is this central power, this vital part, called the soul. And it is on this that we must concentrate our attention.

Bearing that picture in mind, let us now see what the gospel has to say about life. The first principle is, that face to face with the problems of life there is only one thing that needs to be examined—namely, the eye, the centre, the soul. In view of the fact that the light of the body is the eye, the only thing that needs to be examined is the eye, for if the eye is single the whole body will be full of light. But if the eye is evil the whole body will be full of darkness. Everything therefore depends upon the eye. The condition of the

[1] Luke xi. 34.

eye is the one thing that matters, and our Lord goes on to add the solemn warning in the next verse, "Take heed therefore that the light which is in thee be not darkness."[1] How masterly is the gospel, and how thoroughly it knows us! How direct it is in its approach! Ignoring the trivialities and the non-essentials, it comes at once to the heart of the matter.

This direct simplicity is perfectly illustrated in many places in the Scripture, and most conveniently for reference, in an incident which followed immediately after our Lord had spoken the above words. He went in at the request of a certain Pharisee to dine in his house, and at once sat down to meat. The Pharisee observing His act was surprised, marvelling that Christ had not first washed before dinner. You remember our Lord's answer to him. He turned to him and delivered a stern denunciation of the Pharisees and their ways and views. They who were so careful about the outside of the cup and the platter forgot the inside, which was infinitely more important. They were experts on externals and non-essentials, but were ignorant of the one thing that mattered. They kept rules and regulations; they observed great ceremony and ritual. They were experts in minutiæ. They tithed mint and rue, but they passed over judgment and the

[1] Luke xi. 35.

83

love of God. They knew all about the things that were on the circumference of the law, but they were ignorant of its very object, which was to glorify God. As He told them elsewhere, they were sticklers for the letter of the law but were ignorant of its spirit. With their lips they honoured God, but their heart was far from Him. This may be used as a typical example of the way in which the gospel examines the problem of man. It is concerned about one thing only, the soul. Though a man may be right in many respects, as the Pharisees most certainly were, it is all of no avail if he is wrong in the centre, in the eye, in the soul. For if he is at fault there, what appears to be light is nothing but terrible darkness, the more sinister because it appears to be light. It is the eye alone that matters. The gospel has but one test to apply in the first instance.

How sadly is this truth being ignored at the present time. How different are the tests that men apply from what we find here! For we have forgotten that great dictum about the unity of the human personality. We tend to forget the man himself in our interest in his various parts, and the various phases of his life and activities. It is not surprising that mankind is in its present muddle, and that all its attempts at curing its ills are ever hopeless failures; for man does not even know how to examine the situation, much less how to treat it. How numerous are the questions that men ask! How wide is their field of investigation, and how conflicting their opinions as to what really is the matter! They continue to examine, search, investigate, and to apply their treatments; but the muddle still persists. Some, like the Pharisees of old, are simply concerned about outward appearances. The only test they apply is that of outward morality and respectability. To others the one all-important question is the view which we may happen to hold on the subject of war or peace, or on the subject of alcohol, education, or housing. As long as our views on those questions satisfy them, they are agreed that we are Christians; and it is extraordinary to note the zeal and energy, not to say the fiery, warlike spirit, with which they are prepared to preach and to propagate these views. To others, again, the one important question is that of our intelligence and our grasp of certain philosophical principles and ideas. A Christian to such people is, first and foremost, one who subscribes to a certain number of general philosophical propositions. The various schools into which the modern views are divided are almost endless in number. Indeed, they are almost as many as the details of the law in which the Pharisees of old were so expert. A man must be right in this or that respect, and nothing else matters. What an utter travesty of the gospel! How false to its method! For the import is that the various parts of the body are being examined, and not the eye itself, and the eye alone. However, the gospel has but one preliminary test. It is not our outward behaviour, our good deeds. Nor is it our intelligence, our view on some particularly pressing social question. It is not our wealth or poverty, our ignorance or our learning. It is just this one thing. How do we stand with God? Apart from all we are, and all we do, what about ourselves? It is the man himself in the depths, and at the centre, that really matters. The motive is more important than the action. The unseen is more important than the visible. The body is more important than the raiment. The soul is more important than life itself. The vital thing, the only thing that really matters, is how we stand when we are face to face with God alone. Is the eye single? Is it clear? Has the light of God penetrated into and permeated the whole of our being? That is the only point that needs to be determined.

In view of what we have just seen it is quite clear, in the second place, that according to the gospel there is also only one thing to treat. The reason is apparent, and commends itself at once. If the eye is the cause of unruly behaviour, the way to improve the conduct is to treat the eye. I say that that is obvious. I mean that it is obvious to all who have followed the first step, and who have seen exactly what is the cause of the trouble. It is evident to no one else; and there is nothing which is quite so clear in the modern world as the fact that this principle is not being recognized. For the whole basis of society to-day, and especially the basis of many of the most loudly advertised efforts to improve mankind, is upon the opposite assumption. As we have already indicated, the fallacy behind this erroneous thinking is that the man himself is being forgotten, although the different parts of man and his life are being treated. It is assumed that as long as man is put right in this respect and that, the result must be that ultimately he will be entirely right. That is the rationale of the modern belief in what is called the social application of the gospel. It is the basis also of the innumerable societies which clutter the religious ground like mushrooms. It is the background of the belief that by means of greater knowledge and instruction the ills of mankind can be cured. Never has the world been busier in trying to treat itself than it has been during the past hundred years. Indeed, that has been the position for so long that one is tempted, at times, to ask how it comes to pass that the world is ill at all, and needs any treatment, in view of all the advances and development of the past hundred years. How is it that there are any problems left when the golden era began somewhere around the middle of the nineteenth century? But there is no question about the persistence of problems. We have but to look round us to see feverish activity. Leagues and movements against this or that particular sin, organizations to propagate various teachings are to be found on all hands, all under the auspices of famous and learned people. There is not a phase of man's life and activity, but that it is being catered for. His body, his mind, his pleasure, everything. Never was the mechanism for making life happy and enjoyable so elaborate and so perfected.

But what of the result? That question, ignored for so long, at long last is gradually coming into sight. All the effort seems to have resulted in failure, and that for the good reason that we have already considered, that the man himself has been forgotten. He can be put right in many respects and still remain miserable and unhappy in himself. Have we not all known men who are clever, cultured, well-mannered, popular, who, as far as one could see, had everything in their favour, and all that could be desired, but who nevertheless

88

knew themselves to be utter failures in life, and were miserable in themselves? They could manage anyone and anything but themselves. A man may be clever. He may hold idealistic views on most subjects. He may perform many beneficent acts. But the question still is: What are his motives? Is he right at the centre? A perfect illustration of this truth is found in the New Testament in the case of the so-called rich young ruler. There was a man who was right in many different respects; and yet, when he met our Lord, he became convinced that he had a real need and a lack at the very centre of his life. Was not this also the case with Martin Luther before his conversion? He had spent his time in fasting and prayer and sweating. He was trying to put his life in order in a piecemeal manner; and yet, in spite of heroic efforts, he remained centrally miserable and unhappy. But when the glorious doctrine about justification by faith ultimately dawned upon him, and was made plain to him, Luther was put right at the centre and became the mighty reformer whose works we know. John Wesley may serve as another example of the need of a Christ-centre in one's life. There was never a more sincere and honest man. There was never a man who gave such time and energy to the improving of himself. He suffered persecution in Oxford in order that he might preach to the prisoners in the gaols. He eventually gave up his college fellowship and prospects, and crossed the Atlantic to preach to the slaves in Georgia, all in an effort to put himself right. And yet he found that though he had dealt with many aspects and portions of his life, he still remained centrally unhappy and defeated. And then he tells us how, quietly, in that meeting in the room in Aldersgate Street in London, he felt his heart suddenly strangely warmed. John Wesley himself had at last been put right in the centre. His soul had come to that direct knowledge of God which is to be found in Jesus Christ. The eye had been made single, and John Wesley was a new man.

How complex and how complicated is the modern treatment of the parts of man's life! How futile, too, when the central principle is not right. If the eye is evil the whole body also must be full of darkness, however great the struggle to make the different parts light. If the well is poisoned, the stream issuing from it must constantly contain poison, however great the effort to cleanse bucketfuls. James expresses the idea thus in his Epistle: "From whence come wars and fightings among you? Come they not hence, even of your lusts that war in your members?"[1] Or as our Lord

[1] Jas. iv. 1.

reminds us, "Out of the heart proceed evil thoughts, murders, adulteries, fornications, thefts, false witness, blasphemies."[1] What needs to be treated therefore is the centre, the heart, the cause of the trouble and not the various manifestations. Either make the tree good and its fruit good, or else make the tree corrupt and its fruit corrupt,[2] we are adjured by our Lord. Treatment must start at the centre. It is not what man does, or what he knows, or anything about him which needs to be put right but man himself in his fundamental central relationship to God. It is a poor physician who treats the symptoms and complications only and ignores the disease. And the disease is the soiled and tarnished condition of man's soul as the result of sin. His spiritual eye is beclouded and blinded. The light of God cannot enter it. All the darkness within is due to that and that alone. That alone needs to be treated. How simple and direct is the gospel!

Equally true is the statement that if the one thing that needs to be treated is put right the rest will follow. The "therefore" which was used by our Lord brings out this point very clearly. "If therefore the light that is in thee be darkness," He says, "how great is that darkness!"[3] And again, "If thy whole body therefore

[1] Matt. xv. 19.   [2] Matt. xii. 33.   [3] Matt. vi. 23.

be full of light, having no part dark, the whole shall be full of light, as when the bright shining of a candle doth give thee light."[1] "Therefore when thine eye is single, thy whole body also is full of light."[2] Obviously, if the gospel cannot substantiate this claim, all that has been said will be rendered void and useless. The case for the gospel stands or falls by this assertion. This fact has been made abundantly clear in that no line of attack upon the old evangelical presentation of the gospel has been quite so frequent as the charge that it fails to deal with the social problem and conditions. How often has the statement been made that whereas the evangelical preaching of the gospel may be quite adequate to produce personal salvation, it has always failed to deal with man as a social being. But it is a challenge which can be easily refuted, and which is based, either on ignorance of the facts of history, or else upon a wilful and deliberate ignoring of the facts. For the truth is that there is nothing which is quite so glorious in all the annals of the history of the Church in the past, as the way in which this very claim of the gospel has been substantiated and demonstrated. Is it not the simple truth to say that the greatest and most glorious periods in the history of the human race have been those which have followed periods of religious

[1] Luke xi. 36.   [2] Luke xi. 34.

revival and reawakening, when the evangelical truths
of the gospel were emphasized? Such periods as the
Protestant reformation, the Puritan era, and the
great evangelical awakening of the eighteenth century
surely prove this clearly. Can anyone deny that the
movement to give popular education to the people
found its origin in exactly the same impulse? And is it
not a well-known fact that progress in medicine, the
rise of hospitals and the abolition of slavery can be
traced to exactly the same cause? And as advance is
seen in general, so it has been seen thousands of times
in particular instances. Men who have been the hopeless slaves and victims of sin, and who have reduced
their families and homes to conditions of abject
poverty, once they have been converted and brought
to Christ have proceeded to transform their whole
surroundings and conditions. In regenerating a man,
the gospel changes even his personal appearance. He
begins to pay new attention to his clothing and that
of his wife and children; the very furniture of his
home is altered, and the aspect of his premises improved. Once the man himself is put right, he proceeds
to put everything else right. The great movement for
popular education in the eighteenth and nineteenth
centuries came as a direct result of the awakening of
men, under the influence of the gospel, to the realization

of the fact that they had minds and brains. They showed a desire to read the Bible, to familiarize themselves with culture, and to understand life. The number of changes that followed that great spiritual awakening is almost endless. We can illustrate again in terms of a picture. If the source is made pure, the stream is likely to be pure. If the disease itself is treated and cured, the symptoms are likely to disappear.

But we need not state this argument merely in that negative manner as if we were on the defensive. We can be positive, and we can proceed to make the statement that there is nothing else which ever has produced or ever can produce truly improved social conditions except the gospel. Consider the efforts at the improvement of man and the amelioration of conditions that have characterized the past hundred years. But as we have already asked, to what have they all led? In spite of the multiplication of all our efforts, we have but to contemplate our modern world to note that to educate men and give them better houses, does not necessarily guarantee new men or better living. The trouble with mankind is so deep and so radical that it cannot be dealt with in a piecemeal manner. All the problems start at the centre, in the eye, in the soul of man that has become beclouded. And until that has been cleansed there can be no real hope of improvement. But "when thine eye is single, thy whole body also is full of light."[1]

And so we are brought to the conclusion that there is but one treatment which can heal that diseased eye. We need waste none of our time in trying anything else. We need spend no further money on that which is not bread. We can cease to travel round to the various spiritual spas in our search for health and wholeness. The world has done its utmost to clear its own spiritual eye. Patent after patent has been brought out. Lenses and spectacles of all colours, shapes, and sizes have been offered to us, and have been loudly recommended by great and well-known leaders. Often enough we have been assured that, at last, a lens has been found with sufficient magnifying power to enable us to see, and to enable light to penetrate our blind eyes and enter the whole of our being. But still mankind cannot see, and continues in sin and in misery. The strain is too deep. The nebulæ and the mists are not outside the eye but actually within the organ itself. All our own efforts and all our best remedies leave us precisely where we were. Indeed, we find, when we read their biographies or get to know them privately, that the experts themselves

[1] Luke xi. 34.

95

cannot see, and often end their lives, as did the German philosopher Goethe upon his deathbed, with the cry "More light." Can the blind lead the blind? Such men have knowledge in many directions and regarding many phenomena, but at the centre they are all as blind as others. The stain of sin is so deep that the strongest acids known to mankind cannot erase it. Is all hopeless? Is there no cure? Are we all doomed therefore to perpetual blindness and darkness? There is but one hope. There is but one answer. There is but one cure. According to the gospel, Jesus of Nazareth was the only begotten Son of God. He came down to earth because of the blindness of mankind, because man had been deluded by the god of this world. He came and brought that treatment which alone can avail. He has removed by His sacrificial, atoning death and His resurrection the stain of the guilt of sin. He has given new life and power to our diseased and paralysed spiritual optic nerves. He enables us to see God, to behold our Father's face. And, looking at Him, the light of the eternal countenance irradiates our whole being. He said, "I am the way, the truth, and the life: no man cometh unto the Father, but by me."[1] And that statement has been verified in countless thousands of experiences. He said that He was "the light of the

[1] John xiv. 6.

world"[1] and that anyone who followed Him need no longer walk in darkness, but have the "light of life."[2] It is He alone who can reconcile us to God, and enable us to see and to know God. The message of the gospel therefore to this modern, distracted world is that in simplicity it has but to offer this prayer:

> Holy Spirit, truth divine,
> Dawn upon this soul of mine,
> Word of God and inward light,
> Wake my spirit, clear my sight.

It states with assurance that all who offer that prayer, in sincerity and truth, will be able to say with the Apostle Paul that "the light of the knowledge of the glory of God in the face of Jesus Christ"[3] has shined into their hearts.

[1] John viii. 12.　　　[2] John viii. 12.　　　[3] 2 Cor. iv. 6.

CHAPTER FIVE

IS THE GOSPEL STILL RELEVANT?

THE GOSPEL OF JESUS CHRIST CONFRONTS AND CHAL-lenges the modern world with the statement that it alone has the answer to all man's questions and the solution to all his problems. In a world that is seeking a way out of its tragedy and its troubles, the gospel announces that the solution is already available. In a world that is feverishly looking to the future, and talking about plans for the future, the gospel proclaims that the search is not only mistaken in direction, but is also quite unnecessary. It denounces the fatal habit of pinning our hopes to something that is going to happen, and announces that all that is needed by men, individually and collectively, has been at the disposal of mankind for nearly two thousand years. For the central message of the gospel is to tell men that every-thing necessary for their salvation is to be found in the person of Jesus Christ of Nazareth, the only begotten Son of God. He, it proclaims, is the full and final revelation of God. It is in Him, His life and His teach-ing, that we see what man is meant to be, and the kind of life that man is meant to live. It is in His death upon the Cross that we see the sin of the world finally exposed and condemned. It is through His death that we see the only way whereby man can be reconciled to God. It is from Him alone we can derive new life, and obtain a new beginning. It is only as we receive power from Him that we can live the life that God intended us to live. Indeed, it goes further, and assures us that He is seated at the right hand of God, reigning in power, and that He will continue to reign until His enemies have been made His footstool. The gospel proclaims that the time is coming when at the name of Jesus every knee shall bow, "of things in heaven, and things in earth, and things under the earth."[1] Thus the gospel of Jesus Christ confronts man, and urges him to turn back, to look back at this unique Person who was here on earth nearly two thousand years ago, and in whom alone salvation is to be found.

But we are well aware of the fact that the orthodox idea of the atonement of Christ is highly distasteful to the modern mind. There is no reason that is so frequently adduced to-day for the rejection of the gospel as the fact that it is so old. The average twentieth-century individual regards those who are still Christian as being in that position, either because they are woefully ignorant, or else because they have made

[1] Phil. ii. 10.

themselves deliberately obscurantist and are refusing to face the facts. Nothing, to the modern man, is so utterly ridiculous as the suggestion that all he needs to-day is something that has been offered to mankind continuously for nearly two thousand years. Indeed, he regards it as insulting to be told that he, with all his knowledge and advancement and sophistication, is still essentially in the same condition spiritually, as men have been throughout the long history of mankind. He assumes that anything which is so old cannot be adequate to meet the needs of the modern situation. For this reason the vast majority of people do not even consider it. Anything which is so ancient cannot, they argue, be relevant to-day.

Now, what has the gospel to say to such an attitude and to such a criticism? In the first place, we can show that such an attitude is utterly unreasonable, and is nothing but the manifestation of sheer prejudice. Were it not that we are dealing with the most serious and important matter in life, it would be simple enough to show that there are aspects of this question which are most ludicrous. At any rate, we shall be able to point out that people who thus reject the gospel out of hand, and who refuse even to consider it simply because it is so old, can be convicted of failing to apply their own supposed reason and logic. We shall be able to show that many of their own arguments recoil upon their own heads.

For instance, there is nothing which such persons are so fond of claiming for themselves as that they have what they delight to call an open mind. They like to contrast themselves with religious people whose minds, they tell us, are cramped and confined. They charge us with considering but one book and but one person. They, on the other hand, and according to their claim, have kept the windows of their minds open in every direction; and as the result of so doing they have garnered so much knowledge and information as to make it quite impossible for them to accept the ancient message of the Bible. They claim to have open minds, to be free-thinkers. But, surely, before one can claim that a mind is truly open he must be able to prove that it is open in all directions. That mind alone is truly open which is exposed to the north and the south and the east and the west, to the past, to the present, and to the future. A mind which is deliberately shut in any one direction is no longer an open mind. Surely, therefore, when a man dismisses and rejects the gospel without even considering it, simply because it is old, he is admitting that he has deliberately closed his mind to the past. That is not reason. That is not thought. That is not logic. That is nothing but the demonstration of sheer prejudice. Anyone, therefore, who rejects the gospel on the ground of its antiquity alone has no right whatsoever to claim that he has an open mind.

But we can also show that an individual with this type of mentality is guilty of setting up a false standard in these matters. It is clear that his ultimate and most important criterion is age, not truth. And yet, surely, what is important when we are discussing truth, is not the age of truth, but its veracity. This point can be illustrated quite easily. A man who is a seeker in any respect is a man who speaks in this way. "My object," he proclaims, "is to arrive at that ultimate goal and destination for which I have set out. I am so anxious to arrive at that goal that I am prepared to receive advice and information from anyone or from any quarter where it is available. I care not whether the advice comes from the past or the present, or whether it will come from the future. Anything that helps me to arrive at the goal I welcome and I value." For such a man to inquire as to the age of his informant, or as to the date upon his truth, is surely to introduce an utter irrelevance into the discussion. If I say that that alone can be true which is new and modern, and which could not have been known by those who belonged to the past, then clearly my whole idea of truth is changed, and I have set up a standard which is become more important than truth itself—namely, modernity. Sometimes, of course, the standard of dates and age may be quite legitimate. There are those, for instance, who make a hobby of collecting old furniture. In that case they are, no doubt, more interested in the age of the furniture than in its quality. Now, as long as it is but a matter of furniture we are not disposed to quarrel with those who set up such a criterion. But when we are discussing man and God; when we are concerned about morality, chastity, purity; when we are thinking in terms of life and death, of eternity, and the whole future condition of mankind, surely to introduce this question of age, and of dates, is a pure irrelevance, the intrusion into the discussion of something quite extraneous. Regretfully we must indicate that those who are thus prejudiced against the gospel give the impression that their real concern is not with truth itself, but with being considered modern and up-to-date. Their ultimate interest is not in reality, but in modernity.

As we turn for our final exposure of this prejudice displayed by rejection of the gospel simply because it is old, we turn to science, a realm of which the modern man thinks most highly, and which is most popular at the present time. Much of the case against religion and the Bible claims that it has arrived at its position through the employment of the scientific method of inquiry. It tells us that religion belongs to the realm of the imagination and of fancy, the world of romance and of make-believe. Religion, it affirms, must be put into the category of folklore or the fairy tales, into the whole world of unreality created by fear and fancy. Utterly opposed to this, they tell us, is the scientific method, which is concerned only with facts.

Now, it is not our concern at the moment to argue that matter out thoroughly, but we must indicate at any rate the following points in connection with this argument. One is that the truly scientific spirit is always careful to differentiate between theory and fact, between supposition and truth, between hypothesis and that which can be proved and demonstrated. The true realm of science is that of phenomena which can be seen and touched, felt and handled; and the moment the scientist moves out of the realm of the tangible, he becomes a philosopher with no more authority than any other thinker. Now, one of the greatest tragedies in the world to-day is the way in which theories are being equated with facts, and mere hypotheses are being accepted as truths. Many who disbelieve in the very being of God, and who deny the deity of Christ, the miraculous, and the supernatural, do so on the word of certain well-known scientists who refuse to believe such truths. The dogmatic assertions of such scientists are being accepted as solid facts, though in reality they are nothing but theory. No scientist has proved, or can prove, that there is no God, that Jesus of Nazareth was not in a unique sense the Son of God, and that He did not work miracles. No one can prove that there is no life after death, no judgment, no hell. They can simply say that they do not believe such facts. But their disbelief, however loudly and confidently proclaimed, is not demonstration. There is nothing, therefore, more unscientific than the way in which men and women are thus confusing hypotheses with truth, and theories with facts.

This unscientific lack of discrimination may be demonstrated in another way also. What is the truly scientific method of research? It is almost invariably something like this. A young man who is given a piece of scientific research work is generally placed under the care, and in the charge, of an older man, and he goes to this older man to seek advice. What has the old man to say to the young man? Does he tell him to start by burning and destroying every book that has ever been written on the subject in the past?

No, he does the exact opposite. He advises the young man, before he makes a single experiment, to go to the library, and to read and study all the past literature on the subject, to understand it, grasp it, make full use of it. And it is obviously a wise method. Why should a man waste his time in rediscovering that which has already been discovered? Furthermore, as the young man reads the old literature he will find many fruitful items of information for his own research work. The truly scientific method is not one which turns its back upon the past. It is one which starts with the past, studies it, and builds upon it. In other words, there is nothing which is more thoroughly unscientific than the way in which the average person to-day dismisses the Bible, and the whole of the Christian gospel and the Christian Church, without ever reading the Bible, without being familiar with the case for the gospel, without reading the history of the Church. Whatever else may be claimed for the method of such an individual, it stands convicted as the very antithesis of the truly scientific one.

We thus have been able to show that the rejection of the gospel merely in terms of its antiquity is something which, far from being based on thought and reason and knowledge and logic, is nothing but the manifestation of sheer prejudice against the past.

But someone may object that the modern case is not yet met. Someone may suggest that he agrees entirely that to dismiss the gospel, without even considering it simply because it is old, is nothing but the manifestation of prejudice. But he goes on to suggest that his case is somewhat different. He may speak like this: "I am not a Christian. Though I do not believe the gospel, I think I can prove that my rejection of it is based upon reason and demonstration." And this is the case which he puts forward:

"The more I look at life in every respect and in every department, the more clearly do I see that there is a universal law running through the whole of life. It is the law of growth, of progress, and of development. I see that everything is advancing and moving forward. For instance, I look at my garden in the spring and see the seed that has been sown, sprouting. But the seed doesn't stop at that. It grows, blossoms, reaches its full maturity, and then dies. Likewise, when I take a walk in the country in the spring I see the little lambs gambolling in the fields. But they do not remain lambs. They likewise develop and mature. I observe also in the country the modern farmer ploughing his ground with a tractor. I remember days when men used to plough with horses drawing iron ploughs. I have read of days when men used to plough with oxen drawing wooden ploughs, and in still earlier times I know that men used to dig the ground themselves. These examples are manifestations of the same law.

"Again, I look at the modern city with its amenities, and contrast it with the rude mud huts in which our forefathers used to live. I compare and contrast the modern physician and surgeon with the barber-surgeon of the eighteenth century, and the witch-doctor of still more primitive times and peoples. Ever, always, I see the same law. Indeed, I have but to pick up a text-book on any subject, and to compare it with a text-book on the same subject of some twenty years ago, to see at a glance that there has been a great advance in knowledge and information. Indeed, I compare the way in which the last war was fought with the First World War of 1914–18, and even there I see the same law. Everything in life is developing, advancing, moving forward. It is the universal law of life and of being.

"But when the most vital and important matter of all—namely, man, his problems, and his salvation—is mentioned, you Christians suddenly ask us to reverse that process, to turn back and look to the past for the answers and for the solutions. Your position is utterly irrational. It is like asking a modern man when he is taken ill to reject the help of the latest advances of scientific knowledge, and to be treated by a barber-surgeon or a witch-doctor. It is like asking the modern farmer to refuse the offer of a tractor and to continue to dig the ground himself. You are turning back the clock of time, reversing the essential process found in Nature. You are asking man to commit intellectual suicide. I often wish that I could believe your gospel, and that I could become a Christian, but in view of what I have said it is impossible and would be nothing but an act of sheer irrationality."

Such is the case that is put forward at the present time by large numbers of people. What are we to say to such an argument? We start by agreeing entirely with the facts that have been adduced. It is no part of the preaching of the gospel to deny facts, and the believer in the gospel is not an utter fool. He is aware of the advances which have been made in many realms of knowledge. He is well aware of the developments that have taken place in many departments of life, but still he believes the old gospel. "How do you reconcile these two contradictory positions?" asks the modern man. We do so in the following manner. We agree entirely with the facts, but we believe that we can demonstrate that the argument deduced from the facts is false.

But let us, rather, put this in a positive form. Let us give our reasons for still believing in the message of the old gospel in the modern world. Our first reason for doing so is that man himself as man has not changed at all. All the changes about which men boast so much are external. They are not changes in man himself, but merely in his mode of activity, in his environment. This statement can be proved in many ways. It is, for instance, an accepted fact that the really great classic literature of the world is always ageless and timeless. The reason is that it deals with man as man and not merely with certain aspects of men's lives at certain periods. The Greek tragedies are still being translated. The plays of Shakespeare are always contemporary, for Shakespeare, with his profound insight and understanding, was not simply describing Elizabethan man but man as man. The result is that as we read his plays we feel we are reading about representative modern men.

The case is the same with the Old Testament. It is a very old book, yet its characters are essentially modern men. Look, for instance, at Cain, a man who was so jealous of his brother that he murdered him. Are there no such men in the modern world? Then consider a man like Esau, who seems to have been interested only in food and drink. Are there no Esaus in the modern world? One has but to listen to the conversations of people in the dining-cars on trains, and in restaurants, to discover the answer. Then look at a man like Jacob, a man who was anxious to succeed and to prosper, and whose avarice was so great that he did not hesitate to defraud his own brother. Has Jacob become an extinct type? Then consider David, King of Israel. You remember how one day, seated on the roof of his house, he saw another man's wife. He was pleased by her. He desired her. He determined to have her. And he brought about the death of her husband in order that he might obtain her. Are there no men of that type in the modern world? And we could go on through the entire list of Old Testament characters. In almost every single instance we should be looking at a typical modern man. "But surely," asks someone, "there is some mistake. Have you not seen the modern man travelling in his aeroplane at four hundred miles an hour? Are you suggesting that he is identical with the man who used to travel on foot at the rate of four miles an hour?" But wait a moment. Let us look at the two men. There they go, one at four hundred miles an hour, the other at four miles an hour. The vital question to answer in each case is what is the object of the travelling? The remarkable thing is that it is precisely the same in both cases. The individuals are going to make love, or to make war, or to do business, or they are intent upon pleasure. There is but one real difference between the two men. It is the rate at which they travel to the same goal. What, in reality, is the precise difference between the pride which the modern man takes in his culture and sophistication and the pride of those men who, at the very dawn of history, tried to build the tower of Babel into heaven?

But perhaps we can prove this point most clearly by indicating that modern man with all his cleverness and ability seems to be quite incapable of inventing a new sin. It is no part of our purpose to detract or to derogate from the power and the ability of modern man. Truly, his knowledge and ability are very great. He has succeeded even in splitting the atom. But, nevertheless, it is the simple truth to say that he has been quite incapable of thinking of a new sin. All the sins that are being committed in the modern world you will find mentioned in the Old Testament. Or, conversely, all the sins mentioned in the Old Testament you will find being committed by the modern man to-day. Man as man does not change at all. He still remains the same contradictory person he has been ever since the original fall. That is our first reason for continuing to present to him the ancient gospel of Jesus Christ.

Our second reason for so doing is infinitely more

important. God hasn't changed! And it is when we realize, as we have been trying to show, that man's ultimate problem is his relationship to God, that we see the final futility of introducing this question of age and of dates. It is at this point we see most clearly how fatuous it is to reject the gospel simply because of its antiquity. Someone has well put this point by saying, "Time writes no wrinkle on the brow of the Eternal." Of course, there have been advances and developments, but do these in any way affect the being and the character of God? Does the fact that we have an internal combustion engine, and that we have succeeded in splitting the atom, in any way abrogate God's laws or in any way lessen His detestation of sin and wrong-doing? No, the most urgent, vital question confronting man is still the question asked of old by Job, "How should man be just with God?"[1] Certainly there is a new setting to problems, whether they are economic, political, or educational; whether they deal with the shortage of houses or the proper treatment of strikes. But all these problems are temporary. Behind and beyond them all remains that unavoidable situation in which we shall be face to face with the eternal God, "the Father of lights, with whom is no variableness, neither shadow of turning."[2]

[1] Job ix. 2. [2] Jas. i. 17.

The ultimate problem for man is not himself, his happiness, nor the conditions which surround him while he is here on earth. His ultimate problem is his relationship to God both in time and in eternity; and God is eternal, changeless, absolute. How foolish it is, therefore, to argue that modern man needs a new remedy or a new type of salvation rather than "the glorious gospel of the blessed God"[1] which is to be found alone in our Lord and Saviour Jesus Christ.

Our third and last reason for commending this ancient gospel is that there is nothing better than it, or, more positively, that it is still the only thing in the world which can adequately deal with the problem and the condition of man. Let us agree whole-heartedly with the modern man when he says that he believes always in having the best. The man who does not desire the best is a fool. Let us by all means have the best, whatever it may cost and whatever its source may be. Further, it is true to say that in many realms and departments of life the latest is undoubtedly the best. Let us take but one illustration. Of all the amazing and phenomenal advances which were made in the last war, there has been none which is in any way comparable to the advances that were made in the prevention and treatment of the ills of the physical

[1] I Tim. i. II.

body. We are all aware of the fact that by means of preventive inoculation our children can be safeguarded from the ravages of such diseases as whooping cough and diphtheria. We know, too, how men in the Services, on going abroad, are given a preventive inoculation against typhoid fever. Likewise, we have heard of the new chemical treatment of diseases by means of the sulphonamide drugs, and by the so-called miracle drug, penicillin. These latest advances have been truly astounding. Their potency is not just a question of opinion or of theory; it can be proved statistically. It is a fact, for instance, that in the South African War more men died of typhoid fever than were killed in the fighting. Yet in the last two world wars there were scarcely any deaths from this disease, solely as the result of preventive inoculation. Likewise, we can compare the mortality rate in diseases like meningitis and pneumonia before and since the introduction of these drugs. The change is truly astonishing. There can be no question at all but that in the treatment of the ills and diseases of the body the latest is the best. But can the same be said about the prevention, treatment, and cure of the ills of the soul of man? Is there some wonderful inoculation which can be given to young men and women which will render them immune to the insinuations and suggestions of sin which meet them on the streets, in the movies, in the books and magazines they read? Can they be protected entirely against temptation? Is there some wonderful drug which can be given to a man tormented by an accusing conscience and who is acutely aware of a sense of sin and of failure? Is there a tonic which can be given to him which will strengthen his feeble will, and make him more than conqueror over the enemies that assail him? Is there some magical potion that can be given to a man who on his deathbed realizes his sinfulness and is afraid to meet his God and Judge Eternal?

What are the facts? We have seen already that the case for the latest treatment, in the physical realm, can be proved and established by statistics. But what of this other realm? Let us be realistic and face the facts. In spite of the phenomenal increase in education, knowledge, and culture during the past hundred years; in spite of all the Acts of Parliament that have righted wrongs and mitigated injustices and which have been designed for social amelioration in almost every respect, what are the actual conditions prevailing to-day? The answer is to be found as we look at the striking figures of the increase in juvenile delinquency, drinking and gambling, immorality, marital infidelity leading to separation and divorce. Indeed, the results are to be seen in the whole lowering of the moral tone and level of life in most countries, in the sex mania, and in the increasing tendency to live only for pleasure and superficial enjoyment. The fact is that the modern world is desperately ill, that man is perhaps more unhappy than he has ever been.

There is but one cure for the ills of man. When my conscience accuses me there is but one thing I know of that can give me rest and peace. It is to know that Jesus of Nazareth, the Son of God, who bore my sins "in his own body on the tree"[1] has forgiven me. It is to believe, and to know, that because He loved me and died for me, I am clear of accusation. And, conscious as I am of my weakness and failure, and my lack of power to live a life worthy of the name, I am again driven back to Him. It is only from Him and the power of the Holy Spirit which He imparts that I can be made more than conqueror. And as I contemplate myself lying on my deathbed and going on to meet my Maker and my Judge Eternal, my only hope is that I shall be clothed with the righteousness of Jesus Christ, and that He will take me by the hand and present me "faultless before the presence of his glory with exceeding joy."[2] It is always, and only, in Christ that I find satisfaction. It is only in Him that

[1] I Pet. ii. 24.   [2] Jude 24.

my problems are solved. The world, with all its methods, cannot help me at the moment of my greatest need. But Christ never fails. He satisfies always and in every respect. The more I contemplate Him, the more do I agree with Charles Wesley when he said:

> Thou, O Christ, art all I want;
> More than all in thee I find!
>
> .   .   .   .   .
>
> Just and holy is Thy Name,
> I am all unrighteousness;
> False and full of sin I am,
> Thou art full of truth and grace.

He still remains the only hope of individual man, the only hope for the whole world. Is the gospel still relevant? Is its ancient message still adequate? The answer is that it alone is relevant. It alone can deal with, and solve, the problems of man.

MODERN-DAY PARABLES

by

Mari Jones

IN THE SHADOW OF ARAN

Stories from farm life in the Welsh
mountains which present spiritual
truths in a vivid and imaginative way.

This popular little book has recently
been relaunched in a new, colourful
and compact edition, including a
number of full-colour photographs of
the beautiful countryside surrounding
the author's farm.

*'I am sure that this little book will be a
blessing to all who read it — enlight-
ening the mind, awakening the imagination and moving the heart.'*

D. Martyn Lloyd-Jones

and

IN THE SHELTER OF THE FOLD

A sequel to the above,
by the same author.

*'An excellent publication . . . An ideal
gift for Christians and for many non-
Christians also.'*

Evangelical Times

The Lord Our Shepherd

(Now in its sixth printing)

The author's first-hand experience as a shepherd makes this study of Psalm 23 a truly inspiring book.

'spiritually and psychologically refreshing . . . unique . . .'
(*Peace and Truth*)

'warm, devotional, doctrinal preaching at its best'
(*Grace Magazine*)

'a banquet to the hungry and thirsty soul' (*Banner of Truth*)

'a very inspiring little book' (*English Churchman*)

Jesus — Power Without Measure

Sub-titled 'The Work of the Spirit in the Life of our Lord', this book works chronologically through the life of Christ, studying the role of the Holy Spirit in relation to his life and ministry. A remarkable book, charting relatively unexplored waters.

Wrestling with God

(to appear Summer 1990)

This book is based on four addresses given by Professor Douglas MacMillan at the Annual Conference of the Evangelical Movement of Wales at Aberystwyth. Like the addresses that were the basis for his book *The Lord Our Shepherd* these also were greatly appreciated by all those present and will prove of great devotional and practical value to all readers.

The book deals with the spiritual experiences of Jacob and especially his dealings with God at Bethel and Peniel.

CHRISTIAN HANDBOOK

by

Peter Jeffery

This new handbook provides a basic introduction to the Bible, church history and Christian doctrine. In *one* handy volume it therefore provides a range of information which would otherwise only be found either in much larger and more expensive publications, or in a large number of smaller ones. Written in a plain and straightforward style, it will prove invaluable not only for the new Christian but for all who want to broaden their knowledge of the Christian faith.

- Over 90 illustrations including maps, charts, drawings and photographs.
- A comprehensive index.
- Available in hardback and paperback.

'This is a great little handbook, the best of its kind. Let every church buy a copy for each new convert; it's just what they need.' — Brian H. Edwards in *Evangelicals Now*

'This book is packed with information that every Christian needs to know. It is an ideal handbook for young people, Christians and all who wish to broaden their knowledge of the Christian faith.' — David Barker in *Grace*

REVIVAL

Books by Dr Eifion Evans published by the Evangelical Press of Wales:

THE WELSH REVIVAL OF 1904

A thorough but very readable study of the 1904 Revival, with a foreword by Dr Martyn Lloyd-Jones.

REVIVAL COMES TO WALES

A moving and thrilling account of the mighty working of God the Holy Spirit in Wales at the time of the 1859 Revival.

REVIVALS: THEIR RISE, PROGRESS AND ACHIEVEMENTS

A general survey of revivals and their characteristics, concentrating especially on those of the eighteenth century.

TWO WELSH REVIVALISTS

The fascinating stories of Humphrey Jones and Dafydd Morgan, the two prominent leaders during the 1859 Revival in Wales.

Further titles from the Evangelical Press of Wales relating to the subject of revival:

REVIVAL AND ITS FRUIT

by Emyr Roberts & R. Geraint Gruffydd

Studies on the nature of revival and the phenomena associated with it.

HOWELL HARRIS AND THE DAWN OF REVIVAL

by Richard Bennett; introduction by
D. Martyn Lloyd-Jones

Formerly published under the title **The Early Life of Howell Harris,** this book is an invaluable study of the early spiritual life of Howell Harris and the beginnings of the Great Awakening of the eighteenth century in Wales.

Books on contemporary issues published by the
Evangelical Press of Wales

SOCIAL ISSUES AND THE LOCAL CHURCH

Ian Shaw (editor)

Among the subjects covered by this work are: the Christian and the state, the Christian concern for education, the role of women in the church, social welfare and the local church and mission in today's world.

CHRISTIAN FAMILY MATTERS

Ian Shaw (editor);
foreword by Sir Frederick Catherwood

Here is clear biblical teaching by experienced contributors on marriage, parenthood, childhood and adolescence, the handicapped child, fostering and adoption, divorce, abortion and family planning, and the care of the elderly.

THE CHRISTIAN, THE CHURCH AND DAILY WORK

Gerallt Wyn Davies

In this little book the author looks at biblical teaching regarding work, compares it with society's attitudes, and outlines what individual Christians and the church could do to be of effective help in alleviating the great social problem of unemployment.

CHRISTIAN HYMNS

Paul E. G. Cook and
Graham Harrison (editors)

Over 100,000 copies of *Christian Hymns* have been sold since it was first published in 1977. The warm reception given to it by both churches and the Christian press confirm the view of many that it is one of the finest hymn-books available today.

- Comprehensive selection of 900 hymns.
- Suitable for public worship and informal church gatherings.
- Includes 80 metrical psalms and paraphrases.
- Useful children's section.
- Beautifully printed and strongly bound.

Words editions	**Music editions**
Standard words	Standard music
De-luxe words	Presentation music
Large-type words	(with slip case)

CHRISTIAN HYMN-WRITERS

Elsie Houghton

The stories behind some of the great hymns are often as inspiring as the hymns themselves. This fascinating book takes us 'behind the scenes' and enables us to appreciate much more those words with which we are so familiar. In brief but telling biographies, the author covers a wide range of hymn-writers from the early centuries of the Christian church down to the twentieth century. This popular work comes complete with a valuable index, and has now been reprinted with a bright new cover.

'EXCUSE ME, MR DAVIES — HALLELUJAH!'

Geraint D. Fielder;
foreword by Lady Catherwood

The absorbing story of evangelical student witness in Wales in the twentieth century, a story which includes periods of quite remarkable spiritual blessing.

TO BALA FOR A BIBLE:
The Story of Mary Jones and the Beginnings of the Bible Society

Elisabeth Williams

The authentic version of the world-famous story of Mary Jones and her Bible, vividly retold with a wealth of illustrations. Also available in Welsh.

THE CHRISTIAN HERITAGE OF WELSH EDUCATION

R.M. Jones & Gwyn Davies

A thought-provoking book which provides a bird's-eye view of the Christian contribution to education in Wales, and includes a wealth of material drawn from 18th and 19th century sources relating to the subject. This book will be of interest to all concerned with the progress of the gospel, both in Wales and further afield.

These publications are available from your local Christian bookshop, or in case of difficulty, from the publishers, Evangelical Press of Wales, Bryntirion, Bridgend, Mid Glamorgan CF31 4DX, Wales (postage extra). Catalogues giving full details of all publications and cassettes, in English and in Welsh, are also available from the same address.